EDU CAVE MAN

BOB TWELLS & DAVE COLE

EDU CAVE MAN

ILLUSTRATED BY **ROB MURRAY**

First published 2022 by Wrate's Publishing

ISBN 978-1-8383400-9-4

Copyright © Bob Twells & Dave Cole 2022

The EduCaveman Continuum® is a registered trademark of
EduCaveman Limited.Trademark Number UK000003497402

Edited and typeset by Wrate's Editing Services
www.wrateseditingservices.co.uk

EduCaveman® is a registered trademark of EduCaveman Limited.
Trademark Number UK000003497355

A CIP catalogue record for this book is available from the British Library.

This book is dedicated to all educators up and down the country; educators who every day make a profound difference to the lives of youngsters, and who, despite everything, just get on and teach.

It's also dedicated to our lovely families, who have listened to us, made suggestions and encouraged us as we wrote our book during the UK coronavirus lockdowns, when we, along with the rest of the nation, were also struggling through some difficult and strange times. Thank you!

Foreword

By Sir John Jones

In such troubled times, when schools and educators are faced with unprecedented challenges, Bob Twells and Dave Cole will take you on a fascinating odyssey that will remind you why you joined this great profession, why you come through the gate each morning and how possible it is to build the kind of schools we all crave, and society needs. A world in which people matter more than paper and where the needs of children and staff are at the core of every school's purpose. A world in which, more than anything else, it is the quality of the adults and their leaders that will determine whether a school and the children within its walls can thrive and succeed. A positive world in which traditional school cultures based on standardisation, linearity, control, conformity and compliance will give way to those based on possibility thinking, empowerment, creativity and trust. A world in which coaching and professional development become paramount and leaders encourage alternative thinking by asking more and telling less. As you stand at this cultural crossroads, *EduCaveman* will encourage you to step off the treadmill and consider this road less travelled. It will provide a map to guide you, a moral compass to steer you and the philosophical nourishment to sustain you. Laced with humour and stories, it is crammed with ideas, powerful suggestions and simple yet practical ideas. It will challenge you and make you think, but, above all, it will encourage you to believe that the schools we all seek to create are within easy reach. Great educators are not hard to find, seriously difficult to say goodbye to and always impossible to forget. This book will remind you of the legacy such people leave in the hearts and minds of all those they serve. Billy Connolly said that it is the responsibility of every human being to leave the world a little bit less beige than they found it. This book will leave you energised, enthused and inspired by its warm glow of possibility. If you care about schools and the people within them, then this book is for you.

Contents

Foreword   7

About the Authors   11

About the Illustrator   15

The Aperitif   17

Setting the Scene   27

Chapter 1 — The Negativity Bias & the Cautious Caveman   29

Chapter 2 — Education & the Extreme Negativity Bias   45

Chapter 3 — The Journey Towards Champion Caveman Culture   65

Chapter 4 — Wearing Out Your Shoe Leather   81

Chapter 5 — True North   109

Chapter 6 — The Triumvirate   127

Part I — Be more dog   129

Part II — Waiting for Godot   146

Part III — Silence Isn't Golden…   157

The Intermission - Time-out/Breather/Interlude/La Pausa   171

Chapter 7 - Very telling   183

Chapter 8 - Just Ask…   199

Chapter 9 - The Inner Work   219

Chapter 10 - Playtime   243

Chapter 11 - Time For a Change   259

Ciao for Now…   264

Want to know more?   265

Acknowledgements   267

About the Authors

Bob Twells and Dave Cole have been great friends and colleagues since 2000. As late entrants to the world of education, they share a common philosophy that places people and relationships at the centre – youngsters and adults alike.

With over fifty years of combined experience in education, their work is rooted in reality, whilst brimming with optimism, hope and energy.

With an innate sense of fun and warmth, neither of them has lost their belief in education as a powerful vehicle to promote growth for youngsters, and for those working with them.

Outside of education, they share a common love of family, sport, Cornwall, comedy and mischief.

BOB TWELLS

Bob left school with one O-Level at grade 6 (honestly!) and promptly joined the Royal Air Force. During his eight-year career, he educated himself, represented the RAF in the modern pentathlon at the British Championships, worked on Hercules transporters and Vulcan bombers and was awarded an Air Officer's Commendation for Meritorious Service in conjunction with the New Year Honours List 1977.

Whilst studying at Kingston Polytechnic, Bob was awarded the Brigadier STA Memorial Prize for attainment and best all-round performance by a mature student at the college. He went on to enjoy a thirty-year career in schools, twenty of which he spent as a headteacher.

Under his leadership, Bob's first school won Surrey School of the Year, and he finished his career with another of his schools named as one of the top hundred primary schools in the country. He won South East Region Headteacher of the Year in the National Teaching Awards 2000, and he has been a national judge for the same body since 2008. Whenever he's asked about his career, he proudly explains that his most significant success was creating schools where the staff felt energised, optimistic and trusted, where the school was at the heart of the community and where relationships across the school flourished.

Bob is married to Gill (who works in a secondary school). Their children, India, Georgia and Guy have long since left home and are leading independent lives.

Bob currently works as a teacher recruiter, and he thoroughly enjoys coaching and working with the next generation of educators. He also works alongside Dave as a trainer in a variety of areas, a role he finds immensely satisfying and tremendous fun, especially in the field of Behaviour Management. While working together, Bob and Dave have spent many hours chatting about education. It was during one of these sessions that the idea for this book was born.

DAVE COLE

Having obtained a classical law degree from the University of Exeter, Dave secured a job in financial services. Motivated by people and the desire to help others, it wasn't long before the world of education came knocking. His career fate was sealed after a chance chat with none other than Bob himself. Bob persuaded him to move out of his office job in finance and his pinstripe suit and into the classroom – a move from which he has never looked back.

In 2003, following a PGCE at Greenwich University, Dave secured his first teaching role at Furzefield Primary School. Here, he spent several happy years as a contented caveman under Bob's headship. Gaining valuable experience during this time, as both a teacher and leader, and enjoying his role of leading practitioner of primary mathematics, it wasn't long before Dave, keen to replicate the culture he had enjoyed being part of, spread his wings.

In the years that followed, he worked in a range of school settings in different leadership roles – from SENCo to Headteacher. At the heart of this work sat people, relationships and fun, along with his passion for empowering both children and adults.

In 2016, Dave founded Shine Education and Training, which now operates across the South East and works with teachers, leaders, trainees, schools, multi-academy trusts and governors.

Through various Shine Leadership Development Programmes, Dave has worked with hundreds of education professionals, helping to shape the leaders of tomorrow.

Dave also works as a Trainer, Headteacher Coach and School Improvement Partner. His guiding aim, through a strength-based approach, is to ensure that his work leaves teachers and leaders feeling empowered and energised.

During their different headships and, more latterly, in their work with trainee teachers and school leaders, Dave and Bob have found opportunities to have fun working together. Their time is spent chatting about education, culture and the importance of educators as the backbone of our country.

Dave is married to Victoria (also a teacher!), with sons Harry, Tommy and Toby, who are all at different stages of their schooling.

About the Illustrator

ROB MURRAY

Rob Murray is one of the UK's leading cartoonists. He draws every week for *The Sunday Times* and is a regular contributor to *Private Eye*, *The Spectator* and a wide variety of other publications. Over the last 15 years, thousands of his cartoons have appeared in magazines and newspapers.

Rob has illustrated bestselling books and his cartoons also feature in major advertising campaigns. He has won or been shortlisted for various competitions and awards, including Gag Cartoon of the Year (at the UK Political Cartoon Awards) and Cartoonist of the Year (Scottish Press Awards).

In 2020 — during the Covid-19 pandemic — Rob drew 300 personalised cartoons to lift the spirits of frontline key workers, in what became known as the 'Bottle Moments' project. Six months later, a second version of the initiative focused on children who were home-schooling during lockdown and separated from their friends and teachers. Both projects received nationwide media attention, with Rob appearing on breakfast TV and being interviewed by radio stations and national newspapers.

A lifelong artist, Rob is passionate about encouraging creativity, especially in the young. He lives in Surrey with his wife Carina, his dog Bramble, and far too many ideas!

Rob enjoys working for a variety of clients on a diverse range of projects. To see more of his work, buy an original drawing or commission him for a project, visit www.robmurraycartoons.com

The Aperitif

A very warm welcome and a big thank you for picking up our book – it is very much appreciated. We are confident that you will enjoy it and find it useful.

So, what is the book about and how should you approach it? Simple really, it is about the combined philosophy of two good friends who met through education and have remained buddies ever since. Despite the problems and strains of putting this book together at the height of the Covid-19 pandemic, during the lockdowns and living twenty miles apart, we are still hanging on in there.

Our approach, which is continually revisited throughout the text, is one of encouragement. We want to encourage you to consider alternatives and suggestions to school life and school development and see how they might fit in with your current practice – it's as simple as that.

Throughout our careers, we can honestly say we have had great fun working together in our respective schools. Both of us could look you in the eye and say truthfully that we have enjoyed almost every minute and most days we have spent as teachers and school leaders. We hope this is the same for you, our readers. After all, teaching is a great career choice.

We all need reminding of this from time to time, and we feel sure that the chapters in the book will help refresh your memory. In some cases, where time in the 'trenches' may have shrouded your vision and passion for the job and left you more cynical, you may have to dig a little deeper than most. However, we are certain that whilst reading the book, you will gain the necessary warmth from the text and possibly the vision and clarity to see an alternative approach to current school life.

This book is a blend of theory and good, honest experience. It has not sprung out of a thesis we are currently putting together, and it is important to note that while we hope you enjoy what we've written, we're not looking to justify or validate our approach. It is simply our thoughts on the importance of getting the culture right to bring about a more sustainable approach to school life.

Our understanding is embedded in the thousands of discussions and interactions we have had with each other, staff, children and parents. It's more Open University than highbrow, but our belief is unshakeable. If you get some of the things that we describe in this book right, then we believe that you, your colleagues and, more importantly, the children in your care will be in a better place to find further joy and happiness in education.

Whatever end of the 'continuum' (more of that shortly) you find yourself at, we hope this book will give you the inspiration, opportunity and permission to reconnect with your core purpose and maybe even fan that teaching fire in your belly. We hope that as you read and digest the contents of the following chapters, you will be reassured of our belief that learning is both cognitive and emotional, and that both have their place in modern education. This is a book that encourages its readers to unite because of – and not in spite of – differences.

Of course, during our careers, there has been more than the odd wobble along the way for both of us, which you might expect after a combined five decades of experience. We have been tested, sometimes to the extreme. In fact, some of the situations we have faced have left us frightened, and feeling judged and powerless – hard times indeed. But, like most problematic and challenging times in life, they went away, and, eventually, faded in importance (phew), although they seemed to last an age at the time.

These are not ignored in the book, as we have not written the text as 'perfect practitioners', but as practitioners who have learned from, and continue to learn from, our many mistakes. We now fully understand the importance of approaching school development from a cultural perspective, and the benefits that this can bring.

One thing is for sure, though. During our careers, once through the tough times and out the other side, we took stock. We gathered the troops, listened to them and talked things through. We made use of what we had learned and adapted our approach to future proof us against similar situations.

What we started to realise early on, especially when we were headteachers, was that the solution to most, if not all, issues lay within our school. If we could get the culture right; a culture that encouraged staff to feel trusted, supported, valued and listened to, we could build in loyalty and resilience and create a group confidence that would be shared by the staff, parents and children alike. Think of it as a collective "this is how we do things here".

Certainly, once life had returned to normal, the narrative those wobbles created was added to our ever-growing library of stories that we regularly shared with each other, or with friends, over a beer, or even as part of a training programme we were running. We often laughed at the mistakes we made, or the way we tackled highly charged situations to the best of our ability. This wasn't because we are flippant or unable to see the importance of our roles, but because we have found a philosophy and approach that serves us well, enabling us to do more than just survive. We feel confident this will shine through in the following chapters.

It is an approach based on the premise that we have always known how to have fun, and to laugh at ourselves and each other. We have learned how to trust in others and see the positive in difficult school situations, allowing us to easily put the daily hustle and bustle of school into perspective. Our careers continue to be both joyful and inspiring, and we have enjoyed sharing our experience with colleagues along the way.

Our approach to dealing with difficulties has been strengthened by our ability to live in the moment and focus on the importance of simply being present. This enabled us to quickly put the baggage we were carrying from the previous day into perspective. First thing every morning, we left it at the door as we walked through the school playground and connected with the staff, parents and children. Our core purpose and reason for turning up every day was right there in front of us – we just had to embrace it. Yet this can so easily be overlooked, especially if you are not looking for it, or have not tuned your emotional radar to 'locate.'

Our purpose was reaffirmed yet further throughout the day as we walked the corridors while wearing out our shoe leather and talking with pupils and staff about teaching, concerns and school life. Through experience, we learned to invest time in nurturing important relationships and listening to the school community that surrounded us.

Like all educators, we have always been hard working and strived to be well prepared for the days and weeks ahead. We are organised, positive and ready to go! What teacher could survive without this approach? "It comes with the territory," I hear you cry.

Nevertheless, in any school, on any day and at any moment, things can change with little or no notice. (You will know what we mean!) Of course, over time, we just got used to this uncertainty. It became commonplace and part of the ebb and flow of the days, weeks and terms. In a perverse way, our ability to take an assembly at short notice, cover in the lunch hall or simply take a recorder group without any understanding of notation seemed to add to our enjoyment of the job.

> *"Teaching: You laugh, you cry, and you work harder than you ever thought you could. Some days you're trying to change the world and some days you're just trying to make it through the day. Your wallet is empty, your heart is full, and your mind is packed with memories of kids who have changed your life. Just another day in the classroom."*
>
> (Krissy Venosdale – teacher)

The truth is that most days, if not all, you go home exhausted, and you still haven't completed half the things on your ever-growing to-do list. But you give your time to education selflessly and love being involved. After all, we all went into this honourable profession to make a difference to the lives of young people and, of course, this job gives you endless untold opportunities to do this.

Other than being a parent (a 24–7 position!), what other job allows you to influence a child's behaviour, help them overcome their weaknesses and nurture their strengths, creativity and imagination? WOW! As already touched upon, we want to give you the opportunity to reflect on the importance of your role and to gain or rediscover a sense of pride in yourself and your profession.

Having recently reread the infamous Roald Dahl book *Charlie and the Chocolate Factory*, we were struck by the message on the bottom of Willy Wonka's Golden Ticket. We honestly felt it must have been written for us and the millions of educators worldwide.

"In your wildest dreams you could not imagine the marvellous SURPRISES that await YOU!"

Blimey! This has been our shared mantra, which has been ever-present in our unconscious minds throughout our careers – we just didn't realise that Mr Dahl knew so much about teaching! It was the way we approached daily life in school, especially during the years when we were headteachers.

We recommend our mantra to any member of staff who might think they are in for a straightforward time. School life is vibrant and changeable, and it's important to embrace this. In fact, as teachers, our ability to adapt, adjust and turn our hands to all manner of things, whilst showing resilience, is legendary and comes as second nature. "We can do this, we are teachers!"

With that established and shared, we can now take a moment to acknowledge a kind of busyness that has gradually crept into our schools over the last thirty years. This is not the kind created within the humdrum of the school day, as already explained, but the kind created externally. It's pushed through the door or pops into your email inbox. The repercussions might mean that on occasion, you are distracted from the philosophy you are trying to encourage in your classroom or school community.

We are not stating this to make a political point but to illustrate and give context to the essence of our book. Somewhere, in the midst of the weeks and terms, you might have lost sight of the reason you work in education and go to school. We want to help you strengthen your moral purpose and take small steps, or even large ones, to address the negativity bias that might exist within you or your school.

In the past twenty years, a period in history that has seen the launch of YouTube, Facebook and Google Maps, we have had ten Secretaries of State for Education. Can you name any of them? Their motives are totally unquestioned by us, and, without doubt, these national leaders of education entered the job with enthusiasm, integrity and a desire to improve schools – absolutely! However, reform across education has been the key message of all incumbents and, in turn, this has brought relentless change, sometimes at pace, to most, if not all, educational establishments.

"I have made my choice. I have chosen ambition and reform over caution and settling for second best."

(Estelle Morris, 2001)

"And that's why, as Secretary of State for Education, I'm very clear that this reform must continue ... and there's still a lot more to do."

(Justine Greening, 2016)

Couple this reform with the added increase in public demand for 'better schools', which has often been fuelled by the poor image of them sometimes portrayed in the media, the labels allocated to them in the new era of external scrutiny and the excessive accountability that now exists, and you have establishments that are well and truly on the back foot – or right back in the cave. (More of that in the following chapters.) Inevitably, this has led to initiative overload within schools and a reduction in the time to get involved and attend to the important stuff, the stuff that draws teachers to the profession in the first place. This is the stuff that has given us, and many other educators, joy and inspiration. We see this lack of time more and more as we travel around schools, and it has been a major motivation behind us writing this book.

We were never immune to these pressures. In the last decade of our careers, especially as headteachers, we often spoke about the way we had begun to feel unsettled as leaders, with very little time to consolidate actions or initiatives, or to feel relaxed enough to explore and enjoy the motivation behind our decisions and philosophy, let alone consider the viewpoints or issues of other staff members. Reflection was something we saw in our rear-view mirrors as we left the school at an ungodly hour; we were just too busy carrying out the next major initiative that had been delivered to us to think about anything else.

This book was written to encourage all staff in any role to ponder and reflect on a different approach to school life. We want to help education professionals become more optimistic, energised, confident and enthused as they go about their daily tasks.

We hope that our book may bring the people in our wonderful profession closer together; the very last thing we want is for it to be used to polarise opinion. This book does not intend to trump the art of teaching over the science of teaching, or vice versa. It is about hearts *and* minds, and it doffs its hat to the importance of both evidence-based teaching and intuitive, creative pedagogies.

The heart and soul of this book is the exploration of school culture. Our hope is that you, the reader, can use it as a tool for creating schools in which staff can take joy in their role and contentment in their contributions; schools in which staff are confident to take the steps necessary to create a culture that acknowledges strengths and builds upon them; school communities that encourage all members to support and nurture each other through those long weeks and terms.

We hope that you will find some nuggets that will resonate with you and your beliefs. We hope you will be challenged and see strategies and ideas for a different way of approaching relationships and creating cultural shifts. We all want to be the best we can be, of course we do. We want to give our pupils and our schools the very best of ourselves. It seems, though, that after years of trying to achieve these ends, we have achieved far less. Sadly, in many cases, we have had the opposite effect. Perhaps it is time to be a little more sophisticated in the way we approach improving our educational organisations. This will be an approach that will keep the very best of us where we belong – in front of pupils. Surely, we cannot afford to overlook how we might foster a stronger and more healthy culture – a culture in which we stop forcing educators back into their dark caves with to-do lists as long as their arms.

We hope this book might lead some schools towards becoming more optimistic, energised and adventurous. In other schools, it might just reaffirm the cultural strengths that already exist.

This book is a journey through chapters that you can take in sequence. Alternatively, you might want to check out chapters in isolation. We think the text will support both approaches. Over to you!

Think laterally as you use this book, and see the approach we are encouraging as an education-based version of *MasterChef* or *The Great British Bake Off*, with a subtle difference. We are not telling you how to bake the Victoria sponge or serve the prawns with the avocado salsa. We have no technical challenge in which you follow a list of precise and well-ordered next steps. We are simply providing the kitchen, lots of tools and ideas, and the ingredients. It is up to you how you complete the task, and you have no time limit. There is also no limit on the number of contestants that can join in; this is a book for all members of the school community, from the head chef through to the sous-chef.

While reading through this book, hold in mind the beautiful optimism of the universally loved Winnie-the-Pooh, and the simple message that we think perfectly encapsulates our own.

"Supposing a tree fell down, Pooh, when we were underneath it?"

"Supposing it didn't," said Pooh.

After careful thought, Piglet was comforted by this.

Enjoy!

Setting the Scene

We would like you to think of the first three chapters as 'the starter'. Here we will set the scene, providing you with the context to the chapters that follow – 'the main course'.

During the initial trio of chapters, we will acquaint you with a phenomenon called the negativity bias; its origin, its relevance to our lives and how it might impact us as educators.

In the first three chapters, we will also introduce you to our model – the EduCaveman Continuum®, which we hope will be a powerful tool in strengthening your school culture. The continuum comprises our four caveman characters: the

Contented Caveman (illustrated on the previous page), the Cautious Caveman, the Cynical Caveman and the Champion Caveman. Why cavemen? Well, it all started with the negativity bias, but more of that in Chapter One.

Our aim is for the continuum to help you identify your current cultural position and, more importantly (during the main course), that the nuggets, considerations and ideas (the EduCaveman 'Pull' Factors) will support you in moving towards, or further strengthening, a Champion Caveman Culture.

At the very least, we hope our book will support you and your colleagues in finding greater contentment or even joy in the amazing jobs you do – day in, day out – as educators for the pupils in your care.

Laugh, smile, explore and enjoy . . .

Chapter 1

The Negativity Bias & the Cautious Caveman

In this chapter, we describe the ease with which we can travel back (westwards) along our continuum, away from our desired goal of Champion Caveman Culture and towards a more cautious approach, meeting en route our Cautious Caveman.

Better to assume the worst and be wrong than assume the best and be wrong. Pessimism will keep you alive, optimism won't.

Laurell K. Hamilton – American novelist

 OVER To DAVE...

One of the things that has always struck me as odd, and a little depressing, is the propensity of some people to focus on the negative. I guess I notice this more than the average person as my natural disposition is so often one of blind positivity and optimism (beautifully captured in Taylor Swift's song *Dear John*). I have been told on more than one occasion that this is a little irritating, which, to be honest, is a fair comment. That said, I'm sure I'm one of many who choose to think this way.

I can't help it, and I don't know why, but this is just the way I am wired. Life has certainly not been a bed of roses, and I've faced my fair share of adversity, but when the chips are down, I can always fall back on my default thinking, which, to quote Oscar Wilde, assures me that, "Everything is going to be fine in the end. If it's not fine, it's not the end."

Over recent years, though, I have found myself developing an antipathy and a growing resistance to phrases such as:

"Assume the worst and you'll be pleasantly surprised."
"Plan for the worst-case scenario and anything else will be a bonus."

"Expect the worst in people and you won't feel let down."

For me, these phrases are utterly counterintuitive and leave me cold. In fact, I can distinctly remember members of my family making disparaging, tongue-in-cheek remarks about my misplaced utopian view of the world. My retorts were just as barbed. "Must be a joy to live in your cynical world!"

Notwithstanding these frequent jibes, I have remained steadfast in my positivity and belief in the goodness of humanity. On reflection, I guess that is why the profession of teaching, for me, was such a good fit; it provided a chance to serve a system that shapes young minds for the good. To me, whether you're working with children in a nursery or enjoying lunch in a bustling university refectory, the sense of hope and purpose is palpable. Where better to deploy some relentless optimism?

We are all in the gutter, but some of us are looking at the stars.

Oscar Wilde

It seems to me that the extent to which people can, and do, dwell on the negatives has grown over recent times. I recall a recent conversation with my father, who remarked just how dysfunctional society had become, especially concerning the continual media coverage of war, murder and terrorism. He asked if it was realistic for me to maintain such a positive mindset in the face of such awful world events. I thought for a moment and replied, "Yes, absolutely."

Whilst I am not denying that humans are responsible for some of the most terrible things imaginable, you can choose what you read, watch and listen to. If you look for it, you'll find a bounty of amazing things happening in the world, which are often driven by some incredible human beings – often to be located in a school near you.

Have you ever noticed that the news and weather on TV will end with a story of hope or positivity? Let's just look at that a little more closely: fifty-seven minutes of bad news and three minutes of good. I'm certainly no mathematician, but in my book that isn't balanced reporting. I wonder if it's indicative of humanity's insatiable appetite for bad news.

Let's ponder another example; if you pick up any local newspaper, the chances are you'll quickly find a heart-warming story about human goodness – charity work, a random act of kindness or a story about an amazing nurse. They're out there in abundance. Contrast this with some national newspapers that seem to commit a huge amount of column inches to covering crime, political point-scoring and marital affairs. Again, it is clear in my mind that bad news and fear sell newspapers.

So, what's my (utopian) point? It is this: you can choose what type of media you consume, but more importantly, you can choose your attitude and the way you approach your day, even when surrounded by endless images and stories of foreboding. I know I always have. You can make a deliberate and conscious choice to make a positive difference to the people that surround you, especially as an educator.

Incredible change happens in your life when you decide to take control of what you do have power over instead of craving control over what you don't.

Steve Maraboli – behavioural scientist and
bestselling author

Of course, I am aware that not everyone has an appetite for bad news. I don't like to generalise; I take folk as I find them. However, the tendency for people to preoccupy themselves with negative stimuli and to react in a rather extreme way to the vicissitudes of life is something I have increasingly noticed.

Let me take a moment to explore my latter point: the seemingly growing propensity for some people to catastrophise. I was speaking to a friend about his appraisal review when he used the phrase "career-ending feedback". I asked a few probing questions and couldn't help but think his line manager had just been offering some helpful guidance on how he might further strengthen his teaching. To me, "career-ending feedback" evokes a more sinister image, such as the horse's head in *The Godfather*. If you've seen the film, you won't have forgotten it...

On the very same day, my wife was catching up with a friend and chatting about the children. Her friend went on to explain that during football training, her son had collided with another child and bumped his leg. Rather valiantly, he had immediately got up and played on. She asked my wife whether she should take her son to A&E to check that he was OK (even though her son had played on for the remaining thirty minutes of the game with no signs of injury). I guess she is a fully paid-up, badge-holding member of the 'worried well' strata, who seem to be an ever-growing group across society; those people who welcome catastrophe at the drop of a hat in order to justify their actions and existence. Who knows?

Then there was the response to a story I was sharing with a group of friends. I explained that my wife, in a very jovial way, had poked fun at me in relation to the growing number of grey hairs in my beard and how I was no longer a spring chicken. This passing comment was received in the spirit it was intended – as a dose of cheeky banter. But here's the interesting bit: one of the chaps gently intimated that this could be the start of the end of my relationship – and he meant it. Personally, I quietly aspire to the silver fox look. Sadly, in my case, on a good day, I only just manage the silver dingo look, but it's such a small thing that I don't even give it the time of day.

It's clear to me that this growing inclination for some people to embrace negative messages and react in extreme ways can result in a rather cautious and gloomy mindset; a mindset that sees the glass as half empty. This outlook is neatly captured in Laurell K. Hamilton's quote at the beginning of this chapter.

Caveman Nugget

Practice wallowing in moments of positive emotion.

This growing awareness compelled me to investigate further. Was it just something I was noticing, or was it an actual 'thing'? Having delved a little deeper, and having read around the subject, it turns out it was the latter.

Let me take you back in time – to 1.8 million years ago (to be exact). Back to the East African continent. This was a time when early Homo erectus, or cavemen as we call them, walked the earth.

Cavemen certainly weren't consumed with our first-world problems. Their main priorities were survival, hunting for food and keeping warm.

OK, let's now imagine that the caveman and his family have spent the morning collecting firewood for the cave. In doing so, they will have expended a good amount of energy and worked up a hunger. Papa Caveman explains to his family that he'll soon be heading off to go hunting, as Ocado are not delivering in their area that day (and Uber Eats are way off being invented). He's just about to leave the cave when he hears some loud and unusual roaring noises outside. As I see it, he's got two options:

Option A: To remain with his family and choose survival. Although he'll remain hungry, he can skip the possibility of being eaten by whatever it is that lurks outside the cave. He can go hunting later when the coast is clear.

Option B: To put himself in harm's way and risk being eaten alive.

Given that survival was a key priority, the caveman would most probably take the former option, which would ensure the continued and successful evolution of his line. Following the safe and cautious route would become second nature, genetically hardwired into the caveman's programming.

This cautious thinking or programming has been widely described as the negativity bias.

So, it would seem to me that the caveman's existence was relatively simple: he hunted when he needed food, he spent time with his family and, to all intents and purposes, he was quite content.

Welcome to the EduCaveman Continuum – the cultural model on which this book is based. [See figure 1 over the page.]

The Contented Caveman is:

- Enthused
- Creative
- Confident
- Motivated
- Positive

He's the kind of caveman you would enjoy spending time with, wouldn't you agree?

However, when faced with the threat of, for example, an attacking animal, his instincts – or the negativity bias – would come to the fore. Our model describes these Stone Age 'push' factors as:

- Survival
- Fight or flight
- Self-protection

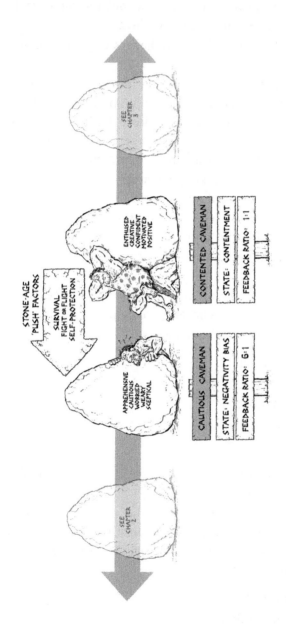

Figure 1: The EduCaveman Continuum – from Contented Caveman to Cautious Caveman

The Contented Caveman moves westerly along the continuum and becomes the Cautious Caveman, who can have the tendency to be:

- Apprehensive
- Worried
- Weary
- Sceptical

Our cultural continuum, as you can see, is an emotional scale – from negative emotions at one end to positive emotions at the other. I've introduced two of our four cavemen here; more from the other two in Chapters Two and Three.

The more eagle-eyed amongst you will have noticed the feedback ratios in our model:

- The Contented Caveman (in his state of contentment) – 1:1
- The Cautious Caveman (with his Negativity Bias) – 6:1

Let's now deal with these. Time to travel back in time again. I'd like you to imagine the Caveman Community. This is a tight-knit group of families who coexist peacefully. Winter is coming and the evening temperature is beginning to plummet. The males of the group work together to collect wood and build a fire. However, it becomes evident that Bob (a Cautious Caveman) is not pulling his weight. Another member of the group, Dave, is aggrieved by Bob's apparent apathy and decides to mention this to him. He's a great friend of Bob's, so he simply asks if he can work a bit harder to help the group. Bob seems to take this on the chin and makes a noticeable effort to up his game. However, he is secretly hurt by the comments and spends the evening stewing over them. He wonders if the other cavemen feel as he does.

I'm positive that, at some point in your lives, you may well have experienced similar thoughts to Bob.

The next day, Dave makes a half-hearted effort to acknowledge Bob's extra input, but Bob doesn't feel the feedback is particularly heartfelt. Another member of the group also celebrates Bob's renewed focus and mentions it to him. Within days, Bob's performance lapses and, yet again, Dave decides to have it out with him and explains how disappointed he is. Consequently, Bob renews his efforts and things get a little better for another couple of days. No one notices Bob's increased output and, you've guessed it, his productivity drops again, but this time even quicker. And so it goes on.

Essentially, Bob does not sustain the required level of performance and lapses to a point that is not acceptable to the group. Research has suggested that to enhance Bob's performance, and address the negativity bias, Dave would need to increase the ratio of praise to negative feedback to nearly 6:1. (Zenger & Folkman, 2013). The social psychologist Roy Baumeister goes a step further and (literally) encourages us to embrace this ideology; in the context of a marriage or a relationship, he suggests that for every breakdown or fight there would need to be five close encounters to restore harmony.

So, just to be clear, to help Bob raise his game permanently, for every piece of negative feedback Dave would need to give six positive comments. (Incidentally, I despise the term 'negative feedback', but more on that later in the book.)

As I've explained, the attributes of the Cautious Caveman have ensured his survival, keeping him safe from danger. But here comes the interesting bit: let's bring ourselves (and the caveman) forward to the present day. The genetic hardwiring of the negativity bias is still present, but the looming threat of a flesh-eating tiger is no longer a reality. By and large, we can assume that survival in our modern world is a given, which then means that the Cautious Caveman's programming is largely superfluous.

So, let's look at the negativity bias in a little more detail, as I think it will shed some light on what I have been noticing over recent years – the fact that people seem to be increasingly preoccupied with negative stimuli and are consequently becoming more cautious.

The negativity bias is widely described as our inclination to embrace negative messages, or things, more strongly than positive ones. Moreover, as well as embracing them more strongly, we tend to linger on them for longer. Have you ever found yourself dwelling on the same issue repeatedly until you become completely subsumed? By which point, as you explain your woes for the umpteenth time, your confidant has left the room without you even noticing.

The negativity bias can also mean that our brains register negative comments far more deeply than a piece of hugely positive feedback from someone we really trust. This point was made in the story about Dave's frustrations with Bob's fire-building apathy.

The Cautious Caveman may well:

- Remember negative comments more vividly than positive ones.
- Remember difficult personal experiences rather than events that have brought deep joy.
- Respond more vociferously to negative messages/ things/events.
- Be more preoccupied with negative things than positive ones.

Caveman Consideration

I would like you to imagine a sliding scale from zero to 10. Zero would indicate a person who is heavily afflicted with the negativity bias, and 10 would denote someone who is largely unaffected by it. On a typical day, where on this continuum would you place yourself? What factors influence this position?

The inclinations listed on the previous page skew the Cautious Caveman's reality and, inevitably, he is predisposed to overplaying the importance of bad things. In contrast, the Contented Caveman is a little more circumspect and can balance up the good with the bad.

The Contented Caveman tends not to dwell or stew unnecessarily on one negative event and can give equal, if not more, recognition to a positive thing or event. Hence, the 1:1 ratio. Moreover, the Contented Caveman will guard against bad events being the platform for his decision-making. The Contented Caveman is sufficiently discerning so as not to let a negative comment be indelibly printed on his memory.

The Cautious Caveman's proclivity to this type of thinking may well have a marked impact on his own life and on the lives of those around him. Let's deal first with his impact on the people around him. Here, I'd like to revisit a phrase I used earlier: *"Expect the worst in people and you won't feel let down."* If your expectations are set this low, it does not bode well for a fruitful relationship. Rather, it creates the ideal breeding ground for disgruntlement and resentment.

I guess meeting new friends may also be a challenge; research shows that the negativity bias can skew perception when meeting potential buddies for the first time, with the Cautious Caveman placing greater emphasis on someone's negative qualities. Sad, isn't it?

In relation to his own life, the Cautious Caveman's rationale for decision-making might also be affected. Risk is a salient factor here; the choices made will inevitably involve an assessment of risk. Should the perceived risk be too high, then the opportunity, whatever it is, may be lost. If we assume there is truth in the saying: *"The greater the risk the greater the reward,"* we can safely say the Cautious Caveman's life may be light on rewards due to his risk-averse nature.

So, there we go – The Cautious Caveman, shaped by his thinking to be:

- Apprehensive
- Cautious
- Worried
- Weary
- Sceptical

As already mentioned, we can assume that survival in our modern world is a given, which in turn means that being overcautious can potentially be unhelpful. So, as you sink your teeth into the following chapters, be mindful of the negativity bias and how, if left unchecked, it can be responsible for curtailing your joy.

So, how is this in any way linked to schools and education? Let's get cracking with Chapter Two

Over to You

Like it or not, thanks to evolution we're hardwired with the Negativity Bias. So, let's make sure we manage it.

Treat it as a lesson – what can you learn?

The first thing is to understand it and then be aware of it in your own thinking. However, be kind to yourself. For the first few weeks, just start by noticing how you react to different events. Don't fight your reactions; just observe your thinking. If you catch yourself dwelling or obsessing on past mistakes or bad decisions, try another approach. Treat it as a lesson and instead see what you can learn. Try to apply this new learning as you move through your professional and personal life.

Chat to a friend

If you continually catch yourself responding negatively to people and events, why not chat to a friend and ask them to check your thinking. Are there good aspects that you have overlooked, which they can help you to acknowledge? Please don't misunderstand me here: I am not for one moment advocating that you neglect to consider the hazards; I am just suggesting that, with help from a trusted friend, you might try and adopt a more circumspect viewpoint that embraces both positives and negatives in equal measure.

Learn to distract yourself

If you find yourself going down a negativity rabbit hole, take action. To disrupt your thinking, do something you love: go for a walk, phone a friend, do some yoga – whatever floats your boat. Manage it: don't let it manage you.

Smell the roses

Don't downplay or gloss over things. Soak them up and linger on them, and then linger on them some more. Share with friends and family. Train your brain to embrace and process positive and negative events with the same weight. Make a concerted effort to set aside time to celebrate, recognise and acknowledge positive things in your life's journey. There's more on this in Chapter Ten.

Capture the positives of the week by writing them down

Grab a notebook and find time to write down the positives of the week. Train yourself to seek them out and then look for ways to share them, where appropriate, with staff, children and parents alike. If you are in a leadership role, perhaps introduce a system to share positive stories from around the school every week.

Just writing for a few minutes each day about things that you are grateful for can dramatically boost your happiness and wellbeing, and even your health. We can also rehearse good news and share it with others...

Alison Ledgerwood – behavioural scientist

Chapter 2

Education & the Extreme Negativity Bias

In this chapter, we'll examine the educational 'push' factors, exploring how they can propel us further west along our continuum and into the cave. We'll consider how these, combined with the negativity bias, move us into the life of our Cynical Caveman. Welcome to the icy world of your very own educational lockdown...

Wanted: A miracle worker who can do more with less, pacify rival groups, endure chronic second-guessing, tolerate low levels of support, process large volumes of paper and work double shifts (75 nights a year out). He or she will have carte blanche to innovate, but cannot spend much money, replace any personnel, or upset any constituency.

Michael Fullan – worldwide authority on education reform

 ## OVER To DAVE

I smiled wryly as I pondered the above quote. I'd stumbled across it several times over the years. Then the smile left my face.

You see, for any school leader, this quote is pretty close to the bone and neatly captures the tension, and reality, that many experience on a daily basis. When I look back on my headships, it certainly rings true for me. More than anything, it makes me reflect on whether I did enough to manage the impact of these pressures on my staff and pupils. Inevitably, some of the incoming workload would be passed straight down the chain, landing on the laps of my teaching staff. And, of course, this more than likely had repercussions for the pupils' learning.

It is hardly surprising then that Contented Caveman teachers and leaders, in the face of growing expectations, can become Cautious Cavemen, who may have the tendency to be:

- Apprehensive

- Cautious
- Worried
- Weary
- Sceptical

OK, let's go a step further and give a little more character to our Cautious Caveman educator. He or she may also be feeling:

- Undervalued
- Dependent
- Disempowered

You'll recall the fire-building anecdote from our first chapter, in which Bob was challenged by his good friend Dave. We learned that to help Bob permanently raise his game and restore his Contended Caveman status, Dave would need to provide Bob with six positive comments for every piece of negative feedback. On this basis, taking teachers or school leaders as an example, we can assume the same: to balance just one piece of developmental feedback would require six pieces of positive or motivational input. You'll notice here that I have deliberately chosen not to use the unhelpful phrase 'negative feedback' and have replaced it with a much healthier alternative – developmental feedback. For me, the choice of language is extremely important, and we'll pick this up again in later chapters.

Caveman Nugget

Who wants to receive negative or critical feedback? Certainly not me! Can we be a little more mindful about the language we use? Why not use the term 'developmental feedback' instead?

So, back to our example. The sad reality may well be that for many schools, a rich culture of positive (four-way) feedback is simply non-existent, or minimal at best. By four-way feedback, I mean:

- Leader to teacher
- Teacher to teacher
- Teacher to leader
- Leader to leader

I haven't overlooked support or admin staff here – at this point, I'm just trying to keep things simple.

It is easy to see how some teachers or school leaders, totally justifiably, let their Cautious Caveman characteristics bubble to the surface.

With all that in mind, it's an opportune time to introduce you to the third caveman on the continuum – the Cynical Caveman. In case you missed him, he was the caveman underneath the stone at the beginning of this chapter.

You will remember that in Chapter One, we described the impact of the Stone Age 'push' factors. In this chapter, I'd like to add some additional 'educational push' factors to the model, which many of you are no doubt familiar with:

- Excessive accountability
- Unmanageable workload
- Initiative overload
- Unrealistic expectations
- Lack of time
- Unbridled 'telling'

The culmination of these additional factors, coupled with the absence of the 6:1 feedback ratio, means that the caveman stumbles further down the continuum – from Cautious Caveman to Cynical Caveman.

At this stage, our Cynical Caveman experiences what we call the extreme negativity bias – a fictional phenomenon created by your caveman authors!

The Cynical Caveman experiencing the extreme negativity bias may feel:

- Judged
- Debased
- A sense of dread
- Uninspired
- Anxious
- Exhausted
- Pessimistic
- Powerless

Incidentally, although our Contented Caveman is not the focus of this chapter, the more eagle-eyed amongst you will have noticed that in this chapter's model we've given him a few more characteristics to account for the continuum's new educational context. [See figure 2 over the page.]

The Contented Caveman educator, as you can see in the model, may also feel:

- Valued/Trusted
- Autonomous
- Empowered

Anyway, back to our Cynical Caveman. In the first chapter, we learned that the negativity bias can be our inclination to embrace negative stimuli more strongly than positive stimuli. We discovered that we have a tendency both to linger on it and remember it for longer. We also learned that the negativity bias

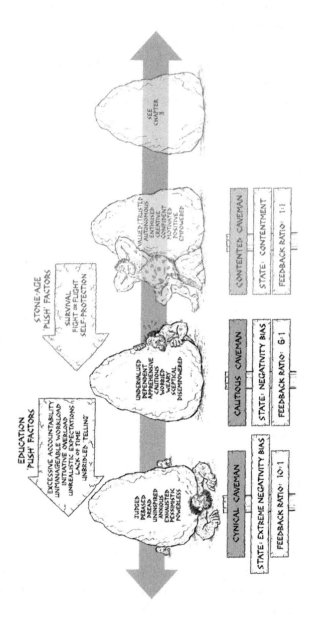

Figure 2: The EduCaveman Continuum – from Cautious Caveman to Cynical Caveman

can mean that our brains register personal and hurtful comments far more deeply than a piece of hugely positive feedback from a trusted friend or colleague.

We said that the Cautious Caveman may well:

- Remember negative comments more vividly than positive ones.
- Remember difficult personal experiences rather than events that have brought deep joy.
- Respond more vociferously to negative messages/things/events.
- Be more preoccupied with negative things than positive ones.

I will now look at each of these four assertions through the eyes of an educator. However, before I do this, I would like to make three personal observations that may help you understand why Cynical Caveman teachers and leaders may be predisposed to this way of thinking and/or feeling.

1. "You criticise my teaching/school, you criticise my very being."

Teaching is in the blood; it's a vocation. Speak to any educator and they will make no bones about the fact that this job is heart and soul stuff; it's deeply personal. If you work in education, the simple truth is that you give it your all, and then some.

The bottom line isn't profit. It's about something far more important than that: life chances. No educator ever wakes up in the morning, ponders the day ahead, and says, "Today I'll aim for mediocrity."

They may well aim for survival, but certainly not mediocrity.

Caveman Nugget

Know this: no matter how exhausting or challenging the day has been, your pupils hugely appreciate the time and love you invest in them – although they might never show it.

Programmed into every educator's DNA is the assumption that every interaction with a pupil could be the one that changes their life.

Educators invest in their pupils, and they keep investing, day after day, term after term, year after year. They back their pupils and they back them some more. They invest emotionally, even when their own emotional wells have run dry. To say that teaching or school leadership is an emotional job is to underplay it.

One looks back with appreciation to the brilliant teachers,
but with gratitude to those who touched our human feelings.
The curriculum is so much necessary raw material,
but warmth is the vital element for the growing plant
and for the soul of the child.

Carl Jung – one of the world's most influential psychiatrists

2. The deficit model of education

Let me transport you back to your teacher training. Remember it? If you were in any way prone to sensitivity this would have been a tough time. I was all too aware of my paper-thin skin thickening as I naively navigated the early months of my training. For me, it was an emotional battleground on which the basis of development and professional growth was a relentless focus on what I wasn't doing and the skills I hadn't yet mastered.

I distinctly recall nailing an ongoing target (ensuring an appropriate balance of teacher talk versus pupil talk) and looking forward to receiving some positive feedback. I was like a child knowing that I would be going to the sweet shop after school. Sadly, the reality was thoroughly underwhelming. Yes, my progress against the target was acknowledged, but for the remaining fifty-nine minutes and thirty seconds of the sixty-minute feedback session, we focused on new deficits. Ring any bells?

Weirdly, or depressingly, I adapted and came to normalise this perverse way of working. Given that I didn't know any different, I just assumed that this was how it was in education. And even after nearly twenty years, it didn't stop – and it still hasn't. Whether you're a teacher or a leader, you'll experience the same phenomenon – from appraisals to pupil progress meetings, from book looks to lesson observations, from governing body meetings to parent forums, and from local authority reviews to health and safety audits. It goes on and on...

If we ask people to look for deficits, they will usually find them, and their view of the situation will be coloured by this. If we ask people to look for successes, they will usually find them, and their view of the situation will be coloured by this.

Ron Kral – author of *Strategies that Work: Techniques for Solutions in Schools*

The common thread running through all these systems? As sure as night follows day, you can be certain to find an unswerving focus on:

- Weaknesses
- Next steps
- Gaps

- Even better ifs
- Missed targets

I began to make a mental note of the time spent evaluating success or strengths compared to the time spent on weaknesses. You won't be surprised with the findings. I like to call this the deficit model of education. It's staggeringly unbalanced, and if we adopted it with the pupils in our care, we would be nominated at the Teaching Awards in the category of Most Demotivating Teacher.

Don't get me wrong, I am not for one moment advocating that we ignore or overlook areas for development. Not at all. I just think we need to be more balanced in weighing them up with the strengths. Each should be given equal weighting. You'll remember the 1:1 ratio of the Contented Caveman from the first chapter and his rosier disposition.

Moreover, and we'll get to this later in the book, surely we need to be more discerning about when to provide developmental feedback? To win the war, it's not always beneficial to wage every battle.

3. Use of helpful language

Connected to this, and a point worth making, is the use of language within the deficit model. If you listen closely enough, educational vernacular is riddled with words such as 'scrutiny', 'forensic', 'inadequate', etc. In fact, if you look closely enough, you'll even see this sort of language in education's Ten Commandments, otherwise known as the Teachers' Standards. The preamble describes the requirement for teachers to be 'self-critical'. Not 'reflective' but 'self-critical'! That's hardly language to rouse the soul or foster encouragement. Or maybe it's just me.

Anyway, with these three factors in mind, we should really get back to the Cynical Caveman and those four assertions. Let's begin with the first one. The Cynical Caveman may well:

(1.) Remember negative comments more vividly than positive ones.

To me, this is relatively straightforward. If we assume there is truth in the deficit model of education, it follows that positive feedback may well be a scarce commodity in the workplace. This being so, it also follows that the Cynical Caveman will remember negative comments vividly; these will comprise a substantial part of his professional diet.

It is, therefore, plain to see why the caveman slides along the continuum from worried to anxious and from weary to exhausted.

With constant high-stakes accountability and unbridled 'telling', the caveman goes from undervalued to judged, from dependent to debased, from apprehensive to full of dread and, worst of all, from disempowered to powerless.

And so, to the second assertion. The Cynical Caveman may well:

(2.) Remember difficult personal experiences rather than events that have brought deep joy.

The Cynical Caveman educator, despite being afflicted with the extreme negativity bias, is still an exceptional practitioner or leader. Not a day goes by when the pupils in their care do not thrive. Even if the Cynical Caveman cannot see it, they have become a lifelong role model who the kids will remember years after leaving school. They have been quietly idolised and have a special place in their pupils' hearts.

Sadly, though, they are subsumed with worry about the possible outcome of next week's external review or how they are going to explain a piece of anomalous data to their governing body. They are weighed down by the way the messages in their appraisal meeting were delivered, last week's lesson observation feedback and the ensuing dread of the pupil progress meeting.

The Cynical Caveman educator, understandably, moves from a state of apprehension to one of dread – a word that turns me icy cold and leaves me thoroughly despondent.

Now for the third assertion. The Cynical Caveman may well:

(3.) Respond more vociferously to negative messages/things/ events.

This, for me, is the easiest one to tackle. It is the most obvious. Outwardly or inwardly, Cynical Caveman educators will often have visceral reactions to negative messages.

Let's imagine they are on the receiving end of a piece of poorly executed feedback. Try as they might, separating the personal from the professional poses a substantial challenge. For educators, this is a tall order – a very tall order. I would like to refer to my earlier point: *You criticise my teaching/school, you criticise my very being.* The person feeding back might as well be insulting the educator's family; that's how deep the emotions of teaching can run. It is, therefore, easy to understand why Cynical Caveman educators may well respond emotionally to less than positive messages.

Given the extent of their personal and emotional investment in the job, they may, understandably, slip from feeling undervalued to feeling judged.

Let's look at the last point. Cynical Caveman educators may well:

(4.) Be more preoccupied with negative things than positive ones.

To help with clarifying this assertion, I would like to remind you of the educational push factors in the continuum:

- Excessive accountability
- Unmanageable workload
- Initiative overload
- Unrealistic expectations
- Lack of time
- Unbridled 'telling'

I would also like you to keep in mind that many educators have leanings towards perfectionism (we cover this more extensively in our Playtime chapter). My apologies if you don't, but please bear with me. I think it's safe to say that the vast majority of the profession are guided by the mantra: If a job's worth doing, it's worth doing well – perhaps even perfectly!

In my eyes, the biggest obstacles to achieving perfection are the six educational push factors listed above. Consequently, educators may feel that they are spreading themselves too thinly and failing to do anything to the standard they would like. The Cynical Caveman educator is at risk of then fixating on this dissatisfaction and trivialising or overlooking their abundance of worthy achievements. As they admonish themselves for not delivering perfection in all expected areas, these cavemen may go from worried to anxious.

Although a fictional phenomenon, as you can see, the extreme negativity bias can be very real for teachers and school leaders. Taken individually, it is not comfortable reading, but collectively, the effects may well be amplified. Collectively, Cynical Cavemen do not make for happy staffrooms, schools or systems. In fact, some of the staffrooms I have visited are the kinds of places where, if you are like me, popping in for a coffee is an art form – you slip in and out in record time, avoiding eye contact and escaping the contagion of the 'dead zone' before it's too late.

The Cynical Caveman culture may well be hard to break, especially when we look at the new ratio of 10:1 (which, again, is a work of fiction from your cavemen authors!). This now assumes that for every piece of 'negative' feedback, there would need to be ten positive acknowledgements to move the caveman back up the continuum. Even if we assume that you are a positive role model, believe me when I say, this is going to be exhausting. It will require the combined dedication and resolve of Mother Teresa and Nelson Mandela. Should you achieve this near-impossible goal on your own, drop us a line and we will nominate you for a knighthood!

Caveman Consideration

Do you receive enough positive feedback (*10:1*) to preserve your Contented Caveman status?

Do you provide enough positive feedback to ensure your colleagues don't slip down the Caveman Continuum?

If the answer to either of the above questions is 'no', why not reflect on this further using our four-way positive feedback model:

- Leader to teacher
- Teacher to teacher
- Teacher to leader
- Leader to leader

Among a group of exhausted cavemen (incidentally, known collectively as a chain gang) is it realistic to hope that there will be enough positive energy to redress the balance? Put another way, can educators with depleted or empty reservoirs of hope find the wherewithal to meet the 10:1 feedback requirement for their colleagues? It's a big ask – a monumental ask.

Houston, we have a problem. In fact, we have more than a problem. We have a recruitment and retention crisis. Our profession, as we all know, is haemorrhaging excellent people. Or, in other words, Cynical Cavemen.

What's more, the Cynical Cavemen who remain may be far from happy and perhaps contemplating their future in education as they sit in the darkness of their cave. As I write, yet more depressing research has just been published that attests to this fact. In a Tes article, journalist Dave Speck reported that lower secondary teachers in England were the most stressed among all their counterparts in the developed world.

In July 2020, the Tes published another shocking article, this time by journalist John Roberts. This detailed the findings of an NAHT (The School Leaders' Union) survey revealing that thirty-four per cent of people leading schools said they would be unlikely or very unlikely to recommend teaching to those outside of the profession. More recently, at the end of 2021, yet another survey of NAHT members found the percentage of deputies, assistant headteachers and middle leaders who don't aspire to headship had risen from forty per cent (in 2016) to fifty-three per cent (NAHT Press Room). Not pretty reading.

None of what I have pointed to here is a surprise, especially to those who work in schools. Of course, our model is based on a huge generalisation, and many schools, hopefully, won't recognise the Cautious or Cynical Caveman characteristics. But for those of you who do, and who may be running on fumes, we hope that the following chapters may go a little way to restoring your Contented Caveman status. Perhaps they may even do more than that – but we'll touch on that in the next chapter.

So, what is currently being done to restore Contented Caveman status? The honest answer is, I'm not entirely sure. We will take a closer look at teacher retention initiatives shortly, but first, I'd like to say a word about mindfulness.

Mindfulness seems to be taking centre stage as a mainstream phenomenon in schools. A helpful definition comes from Jon Kabat-Zinn, who developed the Mindfulness-Based Stress Reduction programme, which helps people to deal with stress, anxiety, depression and pain: 'Mindfulness means paying attention in a particular way; on purpose, in the present moment, and non-judgmentally.'

Many schools are using this practice to support pupils and parents, and to help staff manage the stress of the job and avoid burnout.

I'm a great advocate of mindfulness. I buy into it and practise it when I can. However, are we barking up the wrong tree by using it as a possible system fix for stressed staff or Cynical Cavemen? Possibly.

Does the use of mindfulness techniques address the root cause of the problem – i.e., the six educational push factors – or is it simply a way of managing the symptoms? My strong feeling is that it's the latter. Whilst the benefits of using mindfulness techniques are proven and well documented, are they really helping the profession? If the school system was predominantly populated by Contented Cavemen staff, would the need for mindfulness be as great as it is currently?

I guess what I am trying to say is that mindfulness certainly seems to help cavemen staff. However, I would assert that it's not the cavemen that need the help; it's our system. Whilst educators may gain momentary serenity through mindfulness practice, sadly, the bureaucratic workload will still be there in the morning . . .

Let's look at the other challenge I raised earlier – the teacher recruitment and retention crisis. We've all seen the clever TV adverts designed to incentivise people to take up teaching. Whilst I agree that we need to keep the profile of our profession high through such ads, I feel it's of greater importance at this time to retain the excellent existing staff, many of whom may well be at the end of their professional tether.

In my mind, the only way we can do this is through lasting and meaningful systemic cultural change. As a matter of urgency, we must start taking action to restore Contented Caveman status. Throughout this book, we invite you to help turn the tide, and by restoring greater joy and confidence in our profession, we aim for a more contented workforce. I fear that if we sit back and wait for the system to change, we'll be waiting a long while. Time for cultural action.

But how? In the wise words of Mahatma Gandhi, "Be the change you want to see in the world."

Over to You

In the absence of complete systemic and cultural change, are there any actions you can take to remove the sting from the extreme negativity bias or top up the tank a little? Here are some suggestions.

Create a 'Happy Folder'

Start putting together a personal compendium of positive feedback. Include every lovely message you receive, whether a handwritten note from a grateful parent, an email from a colleague thanking you for going the extra mile or a paragraph from your appraisal review that commends you on the exceptional relationships you have formed with the pupils in your care.

And here's the good bit: schedule regular slots to re-read the things people have written about you and pause for a moment to give yourself time to soak it all up. This was something I did religiously, and I reaped the benefits.

Schedule time to consider and acknowledge your long-term impact as an educator

Let me explain. Our system is, and always has been, geared to ensuring that we focus on our short-term impact as professionals. By this, I mean pupil outcomes – the value, as educators, we have added over the years in terms of pupil progress. Whilst I absolutely agree that this should be one of the key determiners in measuring our effectiveness or otherwise, it is not the whole picture.

For me, the most poignant and powerful moments of professional satisfaction come from what I call the 'tap-on-the-shoulder-in-Tesco moments'. These are the occasions when a pupil you taught many years ago grabs your attention on a Friday night – just as you're clasping a bottle of wine and two ready meals – and speaks fondly of the time you sang a daft song on a school residential. The truth is that I often have no idea what they're talking about and, I'm ashamed to say, I sometimes can't even remember their name. But I really believe that these moments, although pretty informal and sometimes a little awkward, provide concrete evidence of something extremely powerful. This is that as educators, we reside in the memories of many pupils. The words we've said, the time we've given and the care we've shown will have provided motivation and life guidance, and it may well have formed the bedrock on which some of our former pupils will have built happy and fulfilled lives. The sad thing for us is that we often won't know it, but that doesn't mean it hasn't happened. These tap-on-the-shoulder moments are the ones to savour, as they attest to your long-term impact. Ask any educator and this is what drives them: the opportunity to make a positive difference to the lives they touch.

So, why then, do we spend such little time as professionals reflecting and engaging with this important aspect of our working lives? Perhaps it's because we can't quantify these moments...

So, what can we do practically to remind ourselves of the reality of the long-term impact we've most certainly had?

We can start by making regular time to:

- Share our stories of long-term impact.
- Watch and discuss motivational clips about the power of teaching and education.
- Think about, plan and discuss the long-term impact we want to have.
- Connect with former pupils and enjoy hearing about their successes.

Chapter 3

The Journey Towards Champion Caveman Culture

In this chapter, we'll explore the need for deliberate and planned cultural investment that will enable us to break free from both cynicism and caution, as we make our way east en route to Champion Caveman Culture. We'll then open the door to the rest of the book and invite you to pack your bags and get ready for a cultural edu-adventure!

Tededeh

This lovely word from the Palembang language, which is spoken in parts of Indonesia, beautifully describes the experience of leaning back on a chair having overeaten and feeling completely bloated and unable to stand up.

It is often coupled with lifting one's shirt and caressing one's stomach.

 OVER TO DAVE...

I would like to invite you to take a moment, cast your mind back, smile and remember your favourite class. Are they in view yet? The fortunate ones amongst you won't have to think too far back, but for others, this may take a little longer. That said, I know that teachers don't have favourites (honestly!), so let's just say the class that was an absolute joy to teach for every day of every term. I'd wager you can still remember all the names of the pupils in this class.

I would now like you to ponder for a moment on how you would describe this class to a friend. What adjectives would be most befitting? No more than ten, please.

I am going to do the same. Here are mine:

- Fun
- Loyal

- Trusted and trusting
- Autonomous
- Inspired and inspiring
- Adventurous
- Exuberant
- Energised and energising
- Optimistic
- Empowered and empowering

OK, so you've described the class. I now want you to try and describe the culture that existed within this class. Let's make this challenging. Can you do it in one word?

For me, my word would be trust. I trusted them and they trusted me – it really was that simple. We were a tight-knit team and everyone in the class understood their value and how to support one another, especially during challenging times. What was so special about that class, and they might never know it, was the strength they gave me through a testing period in my life. I often marvel at the immense privilege all educators have in creating such strong bonds and trust; it is a truly amazing job.

Back in Chapter One, you will recall me mentioning my fondness for utopian thinking and my propensity to be overly idealistic. Well, I can't think of a better chapter in which to satisfy this inclination. However, before we get going, I just want to make sure that we've got everyone on the bus.

In the previous chapter, I mentioned that not everyone reading the book would recognise the Cautious or Cynical Caveman in their staffrooms or schools. However, please be assured that there is still value for you and your Contented Caveman colleagues in the forthcoming chapters. At the very least, I'd like you to meet our fourth and final caveman – The Champion Caveman. [See figure 3 over the page.]

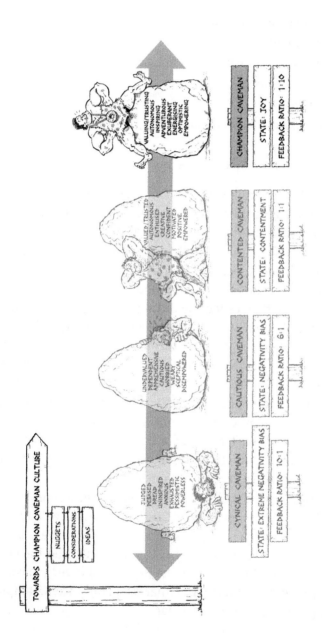

Figure 3: The EduCaveman Continuum – the journey towards Champion Caveman Culture

You won't be surprised to learn that the characteristics of the Champion Caveman are very much aligned with the adjectives I used to describe my most memorable (favourite) class. What I failed to explain is that these were the adjectives I would have used to describe my class in the summer term, at the end of our year-long educational adventure together.

We, not I, worked incredibly hard during the autumn and spring terms to foster and develop this trust. It was the result of many positive emotional interchanges. To be clear, in September, this class was already brimming with delightful pupils. However, with deliberate and planned cultural investment, my class were characterised by the attributes of our Champion Caveman. I am going to overdo the assonance here, but please indulge me. At the end of our journey together, what I was experiencing was the Champion Caveman Classroom Culture!

So, what do I mean by the phrase 'deliberate and planned cultural investment'? Well, that's what you're going to discover in the remaining chapters of our book. The nuggets, ideas, considerations and guidance in each chapter are the pull factors on our continuum. Through embracing or playing with some of our ideas, we hope that, little by little, you will work your way in an easterly direction along our continuum. The contents of each chapter, we hope, will manifest lasting and meaningful cultural change – whether for the classroom, the staffroom, the school or the system.

Oh, and if you're wondering why the Champion Caveman part of the continuum contains an inverted ratio, let me explain (or perhaps it's obvious). If you are well on the road to Champion Caveman Culture, the chances are that you will no longer be preoccupied with the balance of developmental and positive feedback. Your approach will be one in which you are consistently looking for the positives around you. You and your colleagues will deliberately plan opportunities in your day (maybe ten, maybe more) – along the corridors, in the classrooms and maybe even beyond – to get out of your metaphorical caves and find strength. You will find pleasure in acknowledging this stuff and providing positive feedback to your colleagues, smiling as you reap the benefits of the reciprocal trust this builds. Anyway, much more of that later in the book.

Let's be realistic. The journey along the Caveman Continuum may be longer or more arduous for some than for others (for some, the route will be akin to Ikea's endless yellow line), but our hope is that the following chapters will provide some useful and practical guidance (not answers) to help your schools, your staff and your pupils experience the joy of Champion Caveman Culture.

Just to add, as with all these things, this is not a one-size-fits-all book. If you're looking for the silver bullet, then put this book down now (or turn off your eReader!). We simply ask that you take what you like and leave the rest. Whether you're a Cynical Caveman, a Cautious Caveman or a Contented Caveman, there's a worthwhile Champion goal to aim for here. Even if you're not of a perfectionist disposition, you can't deny that aiming for joy isn't half-bad. So, all aboard the Shangri-La Express. Get ready, we're about to take you on a cultural edu-adventure!

Before we push on, though, I'd like to bring some more clarity to the Cynical Caveman's constitution. Having endured the system's push factors (i.e., excessive accountability, unmanageable workload, initiative overload, unrealistic expectations, lack of time and unbridled 'telling') for a number of years, he has sadly become a little... congested, shall we say?

The Cynical Caveman's congestion presents real resistance to the pull factors on our continuum. That said, he just needs a little time and some understanding. So, let's try and relieve some of his discomfort.

The thought of working through yet another menu of initiatives in order to prioritise the next serving is not one to relish. No wonder it can lead to disengagement and a reluctance to get involved. It is of little surprise then that we have some schools full of practitioners who are unable to tackle the next course.

So, what is my point? Teachers are learners, and we just love to learn. Not a week goes by when we are not on the receiving end of a new initiative or trying to embrace a new pedagogy. However, we find ourselves at a frontier; a time when there is a huge focus on the science of teaching, from cognitive load theory to retrieval practice, from evidence-based research to principles of instruction, and much, much more. It is a time when the science of teaching has rarely experienced such clarity. Consequently, schools are awash with pedagogical action plans that rightfully seek to embrace and use these practices for the benefit of their pupils.

However, nothing moves faster than education; if we stand still, in relative terms, we move backwards – rather like walking the wrong way up an escalator. Much of this new practice will, inevitably and understandably, need time to be learned and habitualised. Teachers need to play with it; trial it. They need to make mistakes and experiment.

But given the current high-stakes nature of education, the pressure is on to get it right and to make it part of our teaching repertoire immediately. However, given the push factors, it might be the case that the Cynical Caveman simply doesn't have the capacity to embrace a new habit or practice. Our EduCaveman may be at full capacity just managing every other aspect of the job. He may well be congested; leaning back on his chair, rubbing his head (rather than his belly) and unable to contemplate where he might find time to introduce a new approach.

Our congested colleague may be like those pupils who, by nine in the morning, are already overwhelmed with emotional baggage that will need addressing if they are to embrace any learning in the day or week ahead. Schools frequently go the extra mile for these pupils, deploying a range of exceptionally talented staff to help them unburden themselves of their worries, in the hope that they may then be able to go about the daily business of learning. Sometimes it works and they can, and sometimes their baggage is just too heavy. The point is that, by and large, schools know who these pupils are, and they try and support them so that they are ready to receive. And, most importantly, they don't stop trying. Week after week, these pupils are quietly loved and nourished.

So, with that in mind, let's get back to the congested Cynical Caveman and the key questions I'd really like you to think about.

Caveman Consideration

- Are we maximising the extent to which we can digest and use this wonderful and abundant new pedagogical knowledge? In other words, are we ready to receive?

- What can we do to give ourselves and our colleagues the brain space to embrace something new? If the answer to this question isn't forthcoming, then read on...

As I reflect on the first question, I suspect, regrettably, that the answer our congested Cynical Caveman would give is no. Or, perhaps, as Carol Dweck, a researcher on motivation and mindsets, might say, "Not yet!"

You see, over the years, I would assert that the thrust or essence of school improvement is one-dimensional; it rightfully focuses on improving practice, subject knowledge, resources and vision, etc. Typically, it will include a good old action plan that will come in many guises: a school development plan, a departmental plan, a subject leader plan, etc. If there's one thing we have nailed in education, it is the creation of an impact-focused action or development plan. And interestingly, for the most part, these sit comfortably with the negativity bias: they target weaknesses or gaps (as they should) and often use words like 'scrutinise' and 'forensic'. However, whilst the need for these action plans is undeniable, I wonder whether we can think a little more two-dimensionally?

Caveman Consideration

Who is responsible for the school's deliberate and planned cultural investment?

- How will this happen?
- When will this happen?
- What are the milestones?

My experience of schools is that cultural development is often 'missing in action' and, where present, it is haphazard at best. It is reliant on staff, not plans. It seems to me that Champion Caveman Culture is largely staff-dependent rather than system-dependent. At worst, it is dependent on just one person: a glorified soul, a single point of failure. But what happens to the culture when this member of staff leaves the cave?

Here comes the irony. Having just observed that education is awash with action plans, I am now suggesting that we need yet another one. But don't we?

Well, if our staffrooms, our schools and our system are to support our Cynical Cavemen staff and decongest our bloated EduCavemen, I would emphatically assert that we absolutely need some sort of cultural development plan. With this plan in place, we would begin to see an improvement in the Cynical Caveman's readiness to learn. He would become, dare I say, increasingly willing to receive and more likely to embrace the exciting things on the menu.

The objectives within our traditional school development plan (which would run concurrently with our new cultural plan) would then begin to really take hold. We'd start to see positive movement along our continuum; movement that would power through the continuum's push factors, leaving staff, schools and our education system with a greater sense of empowerment, hope and optimism.

This stuff has to be *explicit.*
It has to be *planned for.*
It has to *be led.*

 NOW OVER TO BOB...

Just a minute, Dave. Before we proceed to the next chapter on our journey towards Champion Caveman Culture, it's important to consider some further factors that may well be holding staff back, leaving them overwhelmed and disillusioned. Factors that, if left unquestioned or unnoticed, might well slow down progress and lead to even greater congestion.

These are factors that we won't be tackling through a written checklist or a specific action plan to fit all briefs. This is because, as we alluded to in the Aperitif, we aren't giving you another lengthy tome telling you what to do; a list of endless strategies or activities that once completed, without much thought or effort, will change your school for the better. You may well have had your fill of this approach.

However, we do acknowledge that throughout life, some activities are best done without too much thinking or engagement. (Reading this book, of course, isn't one of them!) In fact, we've certainly carried out plenty of them in our time. Digging over the garden, cleaning the toilet, sweeping the front drive, etc. We think that, wherever possible, mindless tasks are best kept away from the classroom, allowing space and time for staff to flourish, think and reflect.

When present in schools, mindless activities form a working diet that can be unpalatable and often unhelpful, eventually leading to a slowing down of enthusiasm and positivity. This further clogs up what little spare time was available, ultimately leading to resentment and negativity as you and your team try to complete them. Dare I say it, but these kinds of activities might even have contributed to the increase in the numbers of teachers leaving the profession in more recent times.

My dad Frank used to have a phrase for mindless chores; he said they were the kind of jobs you do with your mind in neutral. These jobs are often tedious and are certainly not the kind of activities you wake up bursting to get on with. And the reason you resent so many of them is because they don't register in your world as crucial, and they might even seem irrelevant to your direction of travel. No doubt you have more pressing and obvious matters to consider within your school or classroom.

Whenever you find yourself tackling one of these tasks, your approach, as you steal yourself to do it, is striking. You tend to complete the assignment in a state of lethargy, with a complete lack of interest or connection to the job in hand. Your aim is simple: to complete the job, tick it off the list and move on. You can then refocus and get back to the day job and your more important work.

Does anything resonate here? It certainly does for us! Too often, we have seen the approach I've just described pulsing through schools, with educators responding to the next demand, the next external barrage. These are the schools where the staff fill their days and weeks completing tasks linked with yet another strategy.

I'd wager that diligent staff in schools up and down the country are simply going through the motions and completing tasks because they must, while seeing little relevance in them to their world or their school's vision.

In the words of the famous Bing Crosby song, it must at times feel like you are *Busy Doing Nothing*.

In more recent times, school days will have been peppered with many of these mind-in-neutral moments, with staff earnestly wading through the next government agenda, policy change, staff meeting and, of course, emails that need an urgent response. Yet this stuff will always be completed, eventually, because teachers are diligent and hardworking. They will be completed if not enjoyed, and sometimes this burden may even be resented.

Subconsciously, we are forcing teachers away from the light and further back into the cave, creating a more cautious workforce and, potentially, a more cynical one, as we exhaust the very people we should be nurturing. Sadly, this may well leave a school de-energised and lacking in enthusiasm.

Yet we all know why staff turn up every morning ready to teach and engage the children; it is the connection, the enjoyment and the opportunity to make a difference. So, why do we allow this depletion of their natural enthusiasm?

The truth is, I don't think we can avoid some of this stuff. In the Aperitif, we touched on the last thirty years of busyness and freely acknowledged how difficult it has been to avoid holding back the surge of initiatives, some of which have led to the eternal to-do list of mindless tasks. In fact, I would go beyond that and say it has been impossible to avoid being touched by this kind of activity. It seems to have affected and afflicted us all. Arguably, no matter how maverick your approach, it has been difficult to resist the ever-changing external agenda. Inevitably, this will make it more difficult to move the school towards a Champion Caveman Culture, as we are so often distracted by the relentless schedule delivered to our door.

To set the record straight, the pressure created by excessive tasks, continual change and overload isn't restricted to teachers in the classroom. It usually starts on the headteacher's desk (as Dave and I both know so well) and permeates from there, depending on the urgency or complexity of the specific task.

Both Dave and I have certainly been responsible for encouraging and supporting the completion of many of these tasks with our respective teams – hours of non-stop fun! We have also been responsible for passing on some (make that lots…) of these tasks, filling up the time of others with myriad mind-in-neutral moments. On reflection, we aren't proud of our mistakes in this regard, but at the same time, we couldn't help doing it, as our own offices were piled high.

Sometimes, working in my office used to feel like being in Harry Houdini's water tank. Like him, I was trying to release myself from my shackles before the water went over my head. I would feel like all I was doing was treading water and losing control of my time. So, as a leader, I would panic and, as the timer ran down, I'd become completely overwhelmed with the enormity of the tasks before me. Rather than drown, I would often take the easy way out and pass some of them on.

A wealth of information creates a poverty of attention.

Herbert A. Simon – American economist and political scientist, awarded the Nobel Memorial Prize in Economic Sciences, 1978

Our ability to sift out mindless tasks became much easier for us later in our careers, as we gained confidence and started to understand the importance of creating culturally aware schools that didn't focus solely on the next idea or the next fad being passed on to us.

Surely, in this time of huge accountability and relentless change, we should be concerned with striking a balance between a systems-led approach and identifying opportunities to truly nurture the school culture? We certainly think so.

We admit that a conflict does exist between the demands of an everchanging education system and the time it takes to create and nurture profound connections (which are the very essence of cultural transformation). Therefore, we don't apologise in our open attempt to stop you looking out from the classroom for the next piece of guidance, or to the school office to receive the next instruction and potentially the next mindless task. *Please, sir, can I have some more?* Instead, we encourage you to focus on looking inward at the importance of nurturing and creating a Champion Caveman Culture within your school – or, should that culture already exist, the fortitude to continue your journey. We see cultural strengthening as the key to a successful school transformation, ensuring that joy and happiness, which currently might be missing in action, return to our profession.

Over to You

If you've enjoyed the first three chapters, why not appreciate the ensuing ones with a colleague, or even as part of a team? After all, it is far more powerful to strengthen a culture with a collective approach rather than an individual one.

**Shared joy is a double joy;
shared sorrow is half a sorrow.**

Swedish proverb

As we mentioned in the Aperitif, we aim for this book to unite our profession. We want to tap into the collective power of working together. So, why don't you start as you mean to go on and assemble your team of cultural attachés?!

Perhaps you could adopt a book club approach: read a chapter and then discuss and review it as a team. Start co-creating your cultural development plan, embracing the ideas you like and discarding those that don't resonate.

Next stop – joy!

Chapter 4

Wearing Out Your Shoe Leather

In this chapter, we'll explore the benefits of being omnipresent and visible in pursuit of positive and nourishing professional relationships.

> *Good relationships don't happen overnight.*
> *They take commitment, compromise, forgiveness*
> *– and most of all, effort.*

Tara Parker-Pope – American author and blogger

 OVER TO BOB...

The quote above was taken from a newspaper article, and while it's aimed at romantic partners, it could equally be applied to any form of relationship, especially those found in schools. This is particularly true when one considers how staff approach the crucial task of building and, more importantly, maintaining positive relationships in all aspects of school life.

In the 1960s, a method of discipline and strict conformity was often used to keep order in the classroom. It was a way of getting through the day both unscathed and untouched by any real connection. Thankfully, times have changed, and building positive relationships plays an important role in any successful school.

We'll go further and say that if learning is to be truly effective and engaging in the modern classroom, a lack of connectedness must not be allowed to hamper the process. Nowadays, teachers and support staff alike utilise the formation of quality relationships in the classroom as their main weapon of choice. These important connections create positive links with children, build up the trust account, allow difficult situations to be tackled more easily and enable every pupil to gain confidence in the learning process.

We do, however, acknowledge that more recently, a zero-tolerance approach to issues concerning poor behaviour, or non-adherence to company policy, has become the norm in some schools. Whilst this may provide a solution in the short term, it avoids the time-consuming yet more rewarding approach of getting to know your audience. Putting in those seemingly thankless hard yards can be tough and labour intensive, but we believe it will reap the rewards in the long run. We will come back to this further on in the chapter. In the meantime, through building good-quality relationships, staff hold the key to successful learning and enjoyment of the learning process, for both them and their pupils. It's worth every single moment you invest.

We are not advocating quality relationships simply as a means of maintaining the status quo. We believe that if used effectively, they are a much more powerful tool and move our EduCaveman out of the cave towards true contentment and joy. When present and effective in schools, quality relationships encourage opportunities for fulfilment, for both staff and pupils. Enter any classroom where they are at the forefront of the experience being offered and you will notice a buzz about the place. The heart of the school will be beating strongly, and warmth will be radiating throughout the classrooms and beyond.

In these schools, every pupil is visible to the teacher, and vice versa. Every pupil is valued and listened to, and, dare I say, so are the staff. They will all be enjoying the collective, positive atmosphere they have had a hand in creating.

I'm just blown away by how kind the teachers are to students here ... but I think that's just a follow-on of the whole culture. You sit in the dining room and you never have to be mindful of what you're saying because everyone's on the same side ... the staff are supportive of each other and I think that carries across into the classroom.

Suzanna Roffey – teacher, educational psychologist, academic and author

For us, positive relationships between all stakeholders (by which we mean anyone who is invested in the welfare and success of a school and its students) and the community are the keystone of any thriving, joyous school. They are a true pull factor in our desire to move out of the cave and actively bring the community closer together. We believe this encourages the school to grow and develop into a motivated, adventurous and happy place to be – a school with an in-built ability to stand solid and assured against any hard times, weathering most, if not all, of the issues it might face.

The subtle difference between our metaphorical keystone and the one used in arch construction is simple. Both are crucial and central to the strength of what is being built. However, the keystone used in constructing arches is often the very last thing fitted, whereas our relationships keystone must be one of the first pieces of the puzzle. Once these quality relationships are in place, building a school community around them becomes so much easier. School development, effective learning and cultural strengthening flourish as a result of the engagement and goodwill of all the stakeholders.

Relationships that are locked and loaded and present throughout a school – in the front office, the corridors and cascading out of the staffroom – are crucial to its wellbeing. They break down barriers, encourage trust and confidence in each other and, more importantly, in the systems and structures that the school is promoting and supporting.

This chapter is pivotal to the ones that follow. Why? Because in the forthcoming chapters, we will be asking you to consider different strategies and approaches, such as listening more and talking less, alternative methods of giving feedback and coaching and learning from each other. These crucial aspects of school life are going to be so much easier to understand when you have a clearer idea about the importance of positive relationships for all stakeholders, and how to go about achieving them.

As we move through the rest of this chapter, we will consider relationships between stakeholders in closer detail, exploring thoughts, ideas and strategies that might help to strengthen these important connections.

Let's start making those connections...

Improving relationships with pupils

I wonder what the response would be if every teacher up and down the land was asked a simple question: "Why do you teach?" I guess the answers would be quite varied, with responses along the lines of, "To get children through the exams", "Because I am paid to", "Because I love teaching", etc. But I wonder what would happen if you were to ask the same professionals what drew them to teaching in the first place. I guess that most of the responses would be more positive and linked to wanting to make a difference.

You see, most of us – although Dave and I would like to think all of us – were attracted to this noble profession by the magnetic force that excited us in those early days in the classroom. We wanted to make a difference to the lives of others, and the prospect of inspiring pupils was at the top of our list. We hope this feeling is still present for many staff, even after years of service. We have personally come across many educators for whom it is. "The force is strong with this one!"

If you were to ask pupils why they enter the school building (something that is rarely done, which is strange, given that they are the 'customers'), you would hope they would say to learn, to have fun and to be part of something. We would be surprised if their answer was: "To be crammed full of information and given new skills and understanding without any connection with the teacher."

Children thrive when the relationships in school are positive and, coincidentally, they enjoy learning more in certain lessons because of the connection they have developed with their teacher. These connections make a difference and, as we all have witnessed in our careers, "the naughty children are never absent". (This was famously pointed out by the late Rita Pierson, an author and professional educator.) We suggest this is because of the connection they feel in your class and the way you make them feel.

Caveman Consideration

Teachers remain important to children *throughout* their lives. If you don't believe us, why not spend five minutes reflecting on a teacher who had a profound impact on your own life.

- What were their attributes?
- What was the relationship like between you?

For us, "Great teachers are like melodies that you can't get out of your head." (The words of a 16-year-old pupil, cited in *The Guardian*, October 2015.)

In a survey, a thousand people were asked to say who had made a difference in their life. Along with parents and friends, a teacher was nearly always in the top three. Each participant was then asked who had had the most detrimental effect on their life. You guessed it: a teacher was generally in the top three there, too. These teachers made students feel undervalued, disempowered and anxious.

We suggest that the teachers at the positive end of the continuum, where I am sure we would all like to dwell, embrace the importance of relationships and spend time listening to and talking with children. At the negative end of the continuum, we find teachers who have slipped into the enforcer role, which is synonymous with the negativity bias. It is, therefore, unsurprising that they are sometimes disliked. The atmosphere they encourage can make students feel anxious, pessimistic and, dare I say it, sceptical.

I've learned that people will forget what you said, people will forget what you did, but people will never forget how you made them feel.

Maya Angelou – American poet, memoirist and civil rights activist

Any gap that grows between students and their teachers can be debilitating to the learning process. I am testimony to that. I left school with only one O-level: a grade six in art. Yet I entered secondary school with an 11-Plus pass and was in class 1A – the top stream of the three forms on offer. In each of my five primary schools (we moved around a great deal), I was a diligent lad who always worked hard (honestly!) and was completely enthused in every lesson.

It is teachers who have created positive teacher-student relationships that are more likely to have the above-average effects on student achievement...

John Hattie – professor of education and director of the Melbourne Education Research Institute

My secondary was a military boarding school, rather like the prisoner-of-war camp in *Stalag 17*, with little hope of any escape or time off for good behaviour. I was homesick and quite sad for most of the time – no, make that all of the time – which is debilitating when you are young. Nobody seemed to notice or care. So, I started slipping (in educational terms) and disengaging with the learning on offer. I began to resent my teachers, eventually ending up in class 3/4G, a small, sad band of brothers aiming for CSEs only (exams you passed for simply turning up to the examination room with shoes on!). This happened within two years of me starting at the school, and because of my poor results in the fifth form, I was asked to leave.

Do I communicate in words and actions that I truly care about and respect and support my students? Research clearly indicates that students who feel cared for and believe they are liked by the teacher will do almost anything, even those odd requests – like adding fractions.

Bonnie Benard – researcher in the field of resilience and youth development

When I left school, I joined the Royal Air Force and proceeded to educate myself by post, attending sessions at night school. To my surprise, I found it all quite straightforward.

Tim Martin, the founder of Wetherspoons, was told by one of his teachers that he would never amount to anything. Tim never forgot the slight and used his teacher's surname when naming his pub chain. (In case you're wondering, he got the initials JD from the character Boss Hogg in the TV show *The Dukes of Hazzard.)*

Caveman Nuggets

If you take nothing else from this book, realise the following:

- Children won't learn from people they don't like or respect. Therefore, it's important that you treat all children with respect and fairness and take every opportunity to develop positive relationships with them.

- Happy children enjoy learning and respond much better to the demands made of them. This isn't rocket science, yet it can be so easily overlooked. We all work better when we are in a good mood.

- You are the big person in the room and should the relationship between you and a pupil break down, it's up to you to fix it. After all, you possess more of the skills required to rectify that situation. Oh, and it's a key part of your job, too!

It is so important to remember that you are the grown-up in the room. By implication, the nurturing of positive relationships is your responsibility. While this may seem an obvious aspect to highlight, and most of you will have it licked, in those difficult moments when relationships have broken down between you and an individual, or even with the whole class, it is up to you to try and fix things, no matter how difficult that might be.

By the way, if something has happened and you have dealt with it badly, and it is appropriate to do so, apologise. This will not be seen by the class as a weakness but as a demonstration of your vulnerability. I have always found that saying sorry goes a long way to strengthening the relationships with my class, so please don't ever worry about uttering that five-letter word. Children will respect you for it.

Caveman Consideration

A percentage of children will feel detached and isolated in class; some may even avoid getting involved and keep their head down. It is your responsibility to notice these children as they begin to disappear off your radar. You need to identify them, find out what is holding them back and put in place strategies to ensure things improve between you.

If you feel this happening, why not try the following:

- Firstly, and most importantly, identify who these children are and ensure you make time every day to form a connection with them. This does not have to be for more than a few minutes at a time, but it must be regular and relentless until the gap has been closed and they feel part of the class culture. If you don't know how to identify these children, then try this: grab a piece of paper and write down the names of all the children in your class or tutor group. You will probably whip through the first ten or twelve, and then you'll start visualising their faces. You can then add the next ten or twelve. But when you get to the last few students, you may have to start wracking your brain. You've now identified your 'under the radar' children – focus on them.

- Notice these youngsters away from your classroom. For instance, if you see them in the dining room, the library or along the corridor, take time to say hello and, if appropriate, have a chat.

- Ask them about their interests and what they enjoy doing in or out of school.

- You could go one step further. If their interest is fishing or dancing, for instance, when you come across an article on that subject cut it out or download it to pass onto them. It's a simple thing that will work wonders.

- Incorporate humour into your sessions. It should lead to a shared positive experience for all the children, helping them to feel at ease and drop their guard.

- When they are on a task and doing well, notice and acknowledge their success. Important connections can be made by something as simple as giving a thumbs up when looking at a child or making a positive comment as you pass their table.

- If they are comfortable with this approach, give them direct praise. Ensure your comments are specific and aimed at something they are doing well rather than general ones.

- Share something of your character (but not too much!). Children feel more of a connection when they know something about you.

Albert Camus was a French philosopher and author who, in 1957, won the Nobel Prize for Literature. He achieved this against all odds after growing up in poverty. He lost his father in the First World War and moved with his brother, mother, grandmother and paralysed uncle to a two-bedroom apartment in a working-class district of Algiers. His mother was illiterate, and he had no access to books in the home.

However, he did have Louis Germain, an outstanding teacher who never gave up on him and, through his kindness and guidance, helped him to gain a scholarship to the Algiers Lycée (high school).

When accepting his Nobel Prize, Albert thanked Monsieur Germain in his speech. Then, immediately after leaving the stage, he sat down to write him a letter to thank him again for his generosity, support and guidance during his formative years. This is what he said...

...when I heard the news, my first thought, after my mother, was of you. Without you, without the affectionate hand you extended to the small poor child that I was, without your teaching and example, none of all this would have happened. I don't make too much of this sort of honour. But at least it gives me the opportunity to tell you what you have been and still are for me, and to assure you that your efforts, your work, and the generous heart you put into it still lives in one of your little schoolboys who, despite the years, has never stopped being your grateful pupil. I embrace you with all my heart...

19th November 1957 (from *More Letters of Note*, compiled by Shaun Usher)

Wow, what an impression Monsieur Germain left on this writer! He clearly had a lifelong impact on the young Camus.

Students spend more than a thousand hours with their teacher in a typical school year. That's enough time to build a relationship that could ignite a student's lifetime love of learning – and it's enough time for the dynamic to go totally off the rails.

Sarah D Sparks – assistant editor, *Education Week*

Incidentally (and somewhat depressingly), while you are busy working hard to develop these important relationships, you often won't get any feedback on how well you are doing. This can be demoralising and reminds me of the years with our three teenage children: grunts and snorts and little else by way of commentary. Measuring this stuff is also difficult, as it doesn't come with a built-in spreadsheet analyser – sorry!

Even worse, sometimes the time, care and affection you show to pupils might *never* be acknowledged. This is difficult to accept, but it's true. Surely, though, this shouldn't really matter given that the essence of teaching is about the giving of yourself, enthusing all pupils and being perpetually optimistic – even to the children you find challenging (and, of course, they must never cotton onto the fact you have put them in the difficult category!).

Our mission is to encourage participation from one and all and show care for everyone in our class or tutor group, which brings me onto an important facet that can often be neglected. It is a known fact that many children will slip through school life quietly and effectively without being noticed. These children are experts at blending in and avoiding contact; they cause you very few problems and always do what is asked of them, never appearing late for anything. Essentially, they are good kids, though they are rarely acknowledged for their consistent, supportive approach. These pupils are your unsung heroes.

These children are the first casualties when the teacher is distracted with the fullness of the day, or when they are dealing with the behavioural issues of the minority. Yet it is so important they know you care about them and value their contribution; they just won't make a fuss if you don't. You need to find a way of ensuring this connection happens, and on a regular basis. Being an average kind of child who goes unnoticed for weeks at a time is upsetting and possibly even demoralising for some children.

You won't be able to avoid involving yourself with the 'naughty' minority (slowly increasing in numbers nationally). That said, some schools have adopted a zero-tolerance approach to poor behaviour. They have a set of consequences to respond to rule breaking, which they never waver from. This can leave them, on occasion, with a waiting list for detention or (even more concerning) with children left in isolation booths for long periods staring blankly at the walls. I have seen that approach used quite successfully on only one occasion: with contestants on *SAS: Who Dares Wins*, a reality TV survival programme...

If a young person fails with English or maths, we put an intervention in place. We give them extra small-group work, or an extra member of staff... whereas if they make a mistake with behaviour, we kick them out.

Vic Goddard – principal of Passmores Academy and star of the BAFTA-nominated Channel 4 documentary *Educating Essex*

Others have taken a markedly different approach. In an interview with *The Guardian* in 2018, Dave Whitaker, then headteacher of Springwell Academy in Barnsley, stated, "We batter them with kindness!" In his school, the staff have an unconditional positive regard towards even badly behaved pupils, and this approach is growing in popularity.

A Review of Educational Research analysis of forty-six studies found that strong teacher–student relationships were associated in both the short and long term with improvements on practically every measure schools care about: higher student academic engagement, attendance, grades, fewer disruptive behaviours and suspensions, and lower school dropout rates.

Sarah D Sparks

If I were a child and needed to feel a connection, was homesick or having a difficult time, I know the approach I would prefer...

So, let's begin our conclusion with the good news. Time after time, research demonstrates that your efforts are noticed and make a huge difference to the way pupils engage in the classroom, with each other and around the school. Who knows, you might even have inspired a career or two along the way.

 ## Caveman Nuggets

It is impossible to know the impact you have on each child's life. However, if you are developing positive relationships with your children you will be making a difference. Trust us!

Get some of this right and you certainly will be named among the top three people who have had a profound effect on somebody's life. You might even have what Dave has referred to as a 'tap-on-the-shoulder-in-Tesco moment', which I reckon has the same status as a Paul Hollywood handshake on *The Great British Bake Off*. It's guaranteed that in these moments, when you turn around, you will be met with a beaming smile and an ex-pupil uttering those immortal words, "Do you remember when...?"

Kids are no pushover, but they yearn to make these kinds of connections, so keep looking to build those relationships, even if it is exhausting at times.

Caveman Consideration

What do you think your pupils want from you when they join you for the new academic year?

Well, when asked, they said it was quite simple. They just want you to:

- Believe in them. Every child wants to feel accepted, trusted and considered part of the class and the culture you are developing (even the difficult ones).

- Support and help them, especially when they are having difficulty.

- Talk to and listen to them. This can be difficult during the fullness of each lesson and the business of the day, but you need to do it. One approach teachers have found successful, especially when they are new to teaching, is to make a list of names in the class or set and tick off the meaningful connections they have made during the week. Towards the end of the five days, you can then prioritise those you have missed.

- Be kind to them. This is so easy to do but it's often overlooked.

- Be fair – always! We know this can be difficult at times, but children do notice inequality. Consider letting them contribute to the class rules rather than just writing a list of dos and don'ts.
- Show them you care. We all like to think that people care about us. Surprise, surprise – students are no different!

It's simple really, but these points can so often be abandoned as you get hijacked by the computer going on the blink, break duty and rushing to meet the next deadline, etc. To me, these bullet points emphasise the importance children attach to feeling a connection with their teacher.

Improving relationships with staff

Positive staff relationships are the bedrock on which happy, thriving school communities are built.

It's worth noting from the outset that these are formed and maintained by the staff regardless of their status and, to date, no external strategy or directive has been created to guide them. Staff who understand the importance of strong relationships in the workplace make meaningful connections across the school and encourage their colleagues to do the same. They are pathologically optimistic and see the best in staff and children alike. This attitude helps them to create schools with a confident, caring and supportive atmosphere, allowing them to embrace the day-to-day business of running a school without being overwhelmed.

Dave and I have come across many schools up and down the country that ooze this kind of positivity. "How do you identify them?" I hear you ask. "What's your criteria?" The truth is, we don't have a particular checklist because this quality is so easy to detect when you are looking for it. You can almost smell it as you drive into the car park.

If you don't believe me, next time you visit a school, have a go at analysing the atmosphere yourself. There's no need for a pen and paper, just start your voyage at the front office and continue through to the classrooms and beyond. In the schools that have nurtured strong relationships, you will notice positivity permeating the building like a breath of fresh air.

The first thing you'll notice in such welcoming schools is the buzz; it's a kind of hum, an energy. These places have a warmth to them; an evangelical openness to share the good news about their school from the get-go.

We believe that if the school is positive and accessible to its community then you can guarantee the children will be on point and the staff motivated and confident. As you walk around, the narrative you'll absorb in the corridors and staffrooms will be optimistic and energised. All the teachers, pupils and support staff will be enjoying the process of learning and the strong relationships they have created with each other.

Caveman Nuggets

Here are some thoughts and ideas for creating a school with positive relationships between the staff:

- Be kind and helpful to all the staff you encounter – from the lunchtime supervisors and volunteer readers right through to the headteacher. You don't need permission to do this, and there is no training course to attend, just get going. If you are already one of these lovely people, then keep up the good work and keep modelling this behaviour. You may not realise it, but many people will be noticing and enjoying your presence.

- When you are at school, be present in the moment, even when you are tired and struggling with deadlines. This will make such a difference to those around you.

- Appreciate others. We are in a business that relies on everybody supporting each other and doing their bit to enable effective learning in the classroom. So, ensure that you always make individuals feel that they are truly appreciated and avoid 'silent praise' at all costs. (More on this later.)

- Be positive and try to see the best in others and in situations.

- Listen more and speak less. (More on this later, too.)

In schools where good relationships are a little harder to detect, the atmosphere lingers like a bad odour – a kind of fog. In these establishments, you might well find that staff are defensive, cautious, wary and pessimistic. Not all at once, and not necessarily in that order, but I think you get the picture.

In the extremely negative schools (and trust us, there are some), where the Cynical and Cautious Cavemen dwell in high numbers, you will find exhausted, sceptical staff who find comfort in moaning about their lot. The staffroom is full of

Dementors (*Harry Potter* fans will know what we mean!), those "dark creatures that consume human happiness, creating an ambience of misery and despair". These people have the power to drain you of your hope and happiness during the briefest of encounters, and even beyond the safe social distance of two metres. (I exaggerate, but you get the drift…)

 ## Caveman Nuggets

If you can't say something nice, don't say nothing at all.

Thumper – *Bambi (1942)*

Staff in these schools, especially the leadership team and the headteacher, have all but disappeared from the corridors and classrooms, avoiding contact with the world of teaching: an outward sign that personal connections are being left to wilt and wither, leading to even further entrenchment and isolation.

Although these schools rarely *fail*, they will never *thrive*. This is because policies, structure and detail (the business documents) have replaced the heart and soul of the building. The leadership has become distracted with onerous bureaucracy and is fully absorbed in tackling the demands this puts on them. Inevitably, this moves them subtly away from nurturing the *soul* of the school towards running the *business* of the school. (We do, however, acknowledge that during the challenging period of the Covid-19 pandemic, tending to anything other than the day-to-day distractions would have been nigh on impossible.)

Dealing with the bureaucracy absorbs so much time, and the ensuing directives are delivered at a relentless pace, often leading to overload, strategy fatigue and even further isolation.

Obviously, we're not advocating that staff should suddenly start hugging and fist bumping, but we strongly believe that if schools concentrate on making profound personal connections, they will be far better equipped to tackle change and introduce new initiatives. This will no doubt have a greater impact on improving the school than yet another delivered directive.

Over the course of our careers, Dave and I have come across so many great staff who enable positive personal connections to flourish. We refer to them as 'radiators' – people who emanate warmth and sunshine.

At the opposite end of the scale, you will find the negative gaggle of staff moaning to anyone who'll listen. We refer to them as 'drains' or 'fun sponges'. These individuals come in all shapes and sizes and will suck away any of the enthusiasm and happiness you arrived with that morning.

Well, the good news is that staff tend to get the school they have created or permitted – the school they deserve. Yes, leadership certainly plays an important role in setting and encouraging the daily tone and modelling the kind of school they have envisioned. However, anybody can contribute, and an all-hands-on-deck approach is most welcome. We encourage you to join in whenever you want; it will make such a difference.

What great news! Whoever you are and whatever your role, you have as much power as the next person to transform the culture of your school. I know this because during my career, I have come across many beacons of positivity. My first deputy head was one such person. She was a leading light who helped to make everyone involved with our school community feel special. My nickname for her was The Angel of the South. Take a bow, Mary!

We heard yet another great example of individual power during a fantastic training day with Sir John Jones, who, you will remember, wrote our foreword. We see him as a true Champion

Caveman. I emailed John to ask for his permission to use the example here. Being the lovely chap that he is, he recalled the story for me in his reply:

"The story to which I think you're referring is when we invited our students to select a mentor from the whole adult community of the school (a big secondary in Liverpool) – someone they liked, trusted and respected, and with whom they could be completely vulnerable in the safe knowledge that that person would always put them back together again. More students chose Joan than any other member of staff, and Joan was a cleaner. She was also the best mentor we had. She had a no-nonsense warmth and unconditional positive regard dripping from every pore in her body. I asked one student, a troublesome, troubled boy, why he had picked Joan. He replied, 'Because when I am with Joan, I just feel good about myself. She can't help me with my work, but she somehow gets me to believe I can do the work. That's gold dust, isn't it, sir?' And that was our Joan, twenty-two carat gold dust. One young girl, who had a history of terrible abuse, answered, 'I picked Joan because when I am with her it's like standing in front of a warm fire in the middle of winter.' That's literally warmth, isn't it, Bob? I hope that helps, and of course you can use it. Our Joan deserves it."

Sir John Jones – keen golfer, former semi-professional footballer, Everton fan and, of course, world-class educator
(sent by email, 6th April 2020)

You see, the significance here is that Joan was the epicentre of positivity and creating meaningful relationships across the school, and yet she wasn't leading anything in the school, except maybe the tribe of children who worshipped her care and kindness. She simply made a difference through her steadfast positivity and warmth.

I feel we need to encourage the 'radiators' in our schools and support every staff member in creating or maintaining a lasting cultural change.

Caveman Nuggets

Surround yourself with *radiators* as often as you can; daily would be great!

Be more like Joan. Remember, you have as much power as anyone in the school to create positive connections – you certainly don't need a title.

Improving relationships as leaders

After leaving the Royal Air Force at the age of twenty-five, I embarked on a BEd degree course. As a student, I was a bit like Tigger. I bounced around on a natural high and got fully involved in all aspects of college life. Having struggled with education so much in the past, now all I wanted to do was learn, and this passion never left me during my entire four years at Kingston Polytechnic (now Kingston University London).

I loved teaching practice, and, in those days, we were assigned annual placements. Most of the schools in the area around my campus were, in essence, middle-class settings. They were great places to gain experience and learn from good teachers. However, by the time I was in the second year, I was after more of a challenge. I wanted my next placement to pick up on the things we were learning about pupils from disadvantaged backgrounds and challenging behaviour, so I pushed my tutor to find a school that would fit the bill. I wanted to see how teachers and staff worked in these establishments, especially regarding how they went about encouraging good learning and direction.

I certainly got what I asked for. The school I was allocated was extremely challenging and in an area of high deprivation. When my friends found out where I was going to be working, some of them suggested taking my gumshield along for good measure!

How naïve we all were. On my arrival on day one, I was a little nervous and anxious, but I was quickly bowled over during my tour of the school. The buzz was amazing and something I have never forgotten. The place was an oasis on the estate where it was located. Everyone who entered felt its wonder, and positive relationships permeated the building.

During my time there, I continued to learn from the wonderful staff, especially Mary, the deputy head and my mentor. My placement there was a real turning point in my professional journey. My skills were moulded, and I developed an understanding of the kind of teacher I wanted to be and the kind of school I wanted to work in. I simply loved it.

But out of all the great staff, it was the headteacher, Derek, who stood out for me. Throughout my career, I have often referenced this forgotten saint, who energised and enthused his staff, creating an atmosphere within the school that was optimistic and adventurous. His relationship with all the stakeholders was exemplary and flowed through the building as he strolled around it daily, modelling the kind of school he had envisioned. I saw Derek all the time – he was omnipresent. At the start of the day, I'd catch him on his early morning rounds, and he'd be visible right through to seeing the children off the premises in the afternoon. Most of the time when meeting staff he would simply chat about things, whether school-related or not, and he always had time to listen. Whenever he was with the children, he again spent time talking and listening to them. He knew all of them, including their families. He always came along on school trips or visits, and he was a strong advocate of being present in the playground. Funnily enough, the only place you could never find him was in his office.

The good-to-great leaders never wanted to become larger-than-life heroes. They never aspired to be put on a pedestal or become unreachable icons. They were seemingly ordinary people quietly producing extraordinary results.

James C Collins – American researcher, author, speaker and consultant

Derek was adored by his pupils and their families. Additionally, the staff were positive, empowered and bonded. I wondered why this was. How was every major issue dealt with so smoothly? Why did the staff turn up with such a great attitude every morning?

The answer was simple and had been staring me in the face from day one – I just hadn't worked it out. It wasn't until the final week that I discovered the secret. I knocked on the great man's door to say goodbye and thank him for a life-changing experience. Before I left his office, I asked him if he could tell me the secret of successful headship. I explained that one day I wanted to lead my own school. He simply smiled and said, "A good leader wears out their shoe leather."

I have never forgotten this simple phrase and have followed Derek's advice in all the schools I have led or been given the opportunity to support. I have also shared his philosophy in the hope that others may pick up on the simple yet effective way of nurturing important relationships. Get out of the office and walk around the school!

Caveman Nuggets

Improving relationships through leadership is about being out and about or 'wearing out your shoe leather'. It's vital to nurture the important relationships that ensure the school is an energised, positive and adventurous place to be. As schools become busier, this is sometimes, and understandably, the first thing leaders ditch to make time for chasing the next target or strategy. Don't be tempted to camp out in your office – start getting around those corridors!

Over to You

Below are some ideas and strategies to foster and strengthen relationships:

- Ensure that the leadership team visits each class at least daily on a walk through the school. Make it clear that this time should be used purely to focus on developing relationships with the staff and students. This could be achieved by designing a simple rota. During the walk-through, whether in the classrooms or corridors, chat to children and staff alike, make connections, find out how they are doing and enjoy passing the time of day. Derek would be proud of you for walking around your glorious school and wearing out your shoe leather, and your staff will feel that you are omnipresent.

- Get to know *all* your staff on a more personal level. Whether it's about school issues or a good boxset on Netflix, it doesn't matter – just get chatting.
- Identify the positive relationships present within your school and, more importantly, those members of staff responsible for creating them (you probably already know who they are). Then encourage these 'radiators' to help you improve connections across the school. Spur them on to radiate their magic wherever and whenever possible. You could even make them part of your cultural attaché team!
- Invest time in developing relationships with parents, particularly the tricky ones; this will pay dividends in the long run. You can achieve this by ensuring staff are visible in the playground, or at the school gate, at the beginning and end of each day. Staff can use these opportunities to spread some good news, either about the school or individual students, especially the ones from the silent majority or who are often in trouble.
- Model behaviours that promote a positive culture across the school. Say hello, smile, spend time with the staff and create opportunities to share yourself throughout the day. Don't get locked in the office dungeon.

Chapter 5
True North

In this chapter, we'll encourage you to reflect on and strengthen your moral purpose in the cluttered world of education.

Turn your face to the sun, and the shadows will fall behind you.

Māori proverb

 OVER TO BOB...

Years ago, my parents decided to move to New York and gave me the task of finding full-time employment and, more importantly, an alternative roof over my head. After a short while and a lot of soul searching, I decided to take the Queen's shilling, follow in my father Frank's footsteps and sign up with the armed services. The one slight difference from my dad was that I chose the Royal Air Force (The Brylcreem Boys) over the army (The Pongos – where the army goes the pong goes!).

Fast-forward six years to the early eighties, and after a lot of hard work, growing up and fun, meet Corporal Twells. (Incidentally, Corporal is the same rank achieved by Spike Milligan in the Second World War and Corporal Jones in the famous TV hit comedy, _Dad's Army_.) I moved around a lot during this time, eventually settling at RAF Waddington in Lincolnshire ('Bomber County'), where I worked as a member of 50 Squadron as a navigational instrument technician.

Our squadron was flying Vulcan bombers: aircraft built in the fifties that were part of the V-Force and still going strong on my arrival at RAF Waddington. It's worth noting that – so folklore has it – the only thing that had been dropped from a Vulcan at this point was a wing panel that became detached over Wales and eventually fell on Tenby High Street. (Our apologies if you were present that day!).

During my time serving with 50 Squadron, we were viewed as a major part of Britain's nuclear deterrent. "Quite a responsibility!" I hear you say. Not to me. I had no clue whatsoever what that meant and how it fitted into the national strategy. Nor did I know what part, if any, Corporal Twells was going to play in the deterrent world. I never once woke up, sprang out of bed and thought, "I wonder if we will be bombing anyone today," or, "I wonder if we will be called upon to deliver a strike against Iceland." (The country, not the shop!) We never spoke about it, and we were never briefed about the implications for our team. It was beyond our immediate culture and moral purpose – it was certainly beyond mine.

We were a compact team of guys with a great culture running through the squadron. We understood our roles and the part we played in the team. We learned from each other and chatted with more senior members about jobs that were unfamiliar to us. In short, we were trusted members of the 'nifty fifty'. I was Corporal Twells, and I knew my purpose alongside my colleagues. We were left to get on with our work with little accountability to others or the need to attend endless meetings or staff development courses – training tended to take place on the job. As a result, we contributed to the squadron's ethos and vision. We were rarely, if at all, affected by external pressures.

Many staff development initiatives take the form of something that is done to teachers rather than with them, still less by them.

Michael Fullan – a worldwide expert in Whole System Change in education and Andy Hargreaves, a researcher, writer, speaker, consultant and policy adviser

I can assure you that we did not waste time sitting around waiting for impending doom. We had far too many things to be doing, and if we found ourselves in a slack period, we would get out the volleyball or sit and chat and enjoy some downtime together.

On reflection, it was apparent that my part in any military campaign, should that time come (read to the end of this chapter for more about this moment) would be like most days, except maybe with greater intensity and longer hours. Why? Because we were an empowered, energised and trusted group of individuals who shared a vision and had confidence in ourselves and in each other. We supported one another during the more difficult times and knew inwardly that we would be ready for any situation that was thrown at us.

After becoming a teacher in the mid-eighties, and throughout my early career, I had a lot of time to do my job and enjoy the process without answering to anyone or being distracted from my core role of inspiring the thirty children in my class. In fact, like my days in 50 Squadron, I was trusted and actively encouraged to be intuitive and creative. Consequently, in my classes, we made silent movies (starring my Volkswagen Beetle!), pinhole cameras, tapestries that were good enough to be hung in Southwark Cathedral, and so much more. I didn't need to justify myself to the head, the staff or the parents. I was the teacher, and it was clear that I knew my worth and was highly valued.

At that time, the school's vision was the only one we followed, and we all understood our roles and how we could contribute to the direction of travel. We knew the school's true north, and this fixed point seldom moved and was rarely, if at all, deflected by any outside interference. We had a great degree of autonomy in the classroom and were rarely affected by initiatives. I am not for one moment suggesting that the education system back then was right or any better than it is now, but it was quite different from my later experiences. My moral purpose could not have been more apparent then; it was right there in front of me – in the form of thirty-odd pupils! I shut the door and I taught to the best of my ability. Distractions were minimal, and I put my training, professionalism and my love of my job to excellent use.

Let's contrast this simple, uncluttered start to my career to my next teaching post, which was, thankfully, just around the corner. Shortly after I started at Moor Lane School, in Chessington, Greater London, the new National Curriculum was introduced and 'attainment targets' became the new buzz phrase. Life became hectic overnight and I have the scars to prove it. The introduction of Ofsted soon followed, bringing with it increased accountability. From the nineties onwards, the educational journey in the UK was strewn with initiatives and ideas. Educators became mesmerised by external strategies and directives, and the added responsibilities these brought.

The thing that struck me as a class teacher, and later as a head, was the relentless nature of these new systems. Looking back, it reminds me of the TV programme *I'm a Celebrity... Get Me Out of Here!*, particularly the Celebrity Cyclone challenge, during which the contestants are pelted with all manner of things while they try and walk up a giant waterslide. Just like in the game, it felt that as an educator, as soon as you got a grip and felt secure and steady, another initiative would come smashing into you, knocking you off your feet.

Throughout that period, it seemed education had become wholly reactive, with schools losing confidence in their direction entirely. The profession was continually reacting to a kind of edu-pendulum, which swung from one extreme to the other, regularly knocking you off-course. As a result, it was much harder to set your own direction and keep faith in your own beliefs.

The briefings for the headteacher, subject leaders and teachers were littered with hot-off-the-press information, sometimes from consultants who couldn't even answer your questions because they'd had no time to digest the implications before passing on the next 'hot potato'. This left most of us playing a guessing game and phoning around to make sense of what we needed to do. I'm embarrassed to say that I did this on more than one occasion. Sometimes, I felt unable to even look for support or advice, as I hadn't fully understood the request. Obviously, this left me feeling anxious, powerless and weary with the hot potato burning a hole in my pocket for days, sometimes weeks.

Some schools began to feel worn down by the continual pressure of this relentless, one-way system. This feeling became even more pronounced if a school's attainment data (an historical way of analysing pupil performance) was insufficient or nearing 'floor targets' – an indicator that your school was vastly underachieving, and you'd be better off reopening as a sweet shop! The pressure was round-the-clock, with headteachers and staff trying strategy after strategy to achieve these seemingly impossible attainment targets. As a headteacher in this position, the day-to-day grind left me exhausted and completely uninspired. Motivating others was something I had to work really hard at, as my mojo had long since fled the building.

A small percentage of schools were so adversely affected back then that the staff, especially the headteachers, started living their lives in the 'waiting room of fear', with their vision paralysed, their heads lowered and their shoulders hunched. Leadership teams were often office-bound; imprisoned by bureaucracy – a similar feeling to that of being egg-bound. The only joy in this pit of despair was the occasional, momentary chink of light after the school had been endorsed by others and judged positively. Then it was back to the grindstone of "We can do even better next time." (See Chapter Ten.)

In those debilitating times, headteachers and staff never seemed to live in the moment or get the chance to enjoy the community they had created. They had lost sight of their vision, and educational direction became more changeable than the magnetic north. Leaders no longer trusted the teachers they had employed to carry the school forward. Staff development became something that was done to teachers rather than with them, to achieve the next target... the next thing on the horizon. This sadly proceeded at a relentless rate.

I'd argue that in some schools today, this culture largely remains in place. In these establishments, the only time you can sit back and relax in the knowledge that things are good and on track is when the external guests have left the building and told you (usually in a later report) that everything "is fine". This period of calm and self-congratulation is generally short-lived. Why? Because at the top of the latest report page are your new targets and a fresh plan for your staff to focus on during the subsequent few terms (and usually at a complete tangent to your current priorities). As the saying goes, there's no rest for the wicked...

This certainly isn't why I used to get up every morning and go to school with a smile on my face, and it isn't the raison d'être we need to encourage in our system. The Champion Caveman won't thrive in a reactive culture that responds to external fads and the next set of instructions. Instead, I suggest we look to create more proactive schools that actively trust and nurture their staff to find their own solutions. Schools that are confident in their culture and sense of direction.

Caveman Considerations

- Innovation and trailblazing in teaching are more aligned with intuition, whims and an unexplainable rationale... or, as we call it, "Great teaching!"

- Be brave with your beliefs. After all, you know your school and its community much better than outsiders.

- Try not to live your professional life in the 'waiting room of fear'; co-create your own plan and momentum.

Getting staff 'on the right seats'

At a conference in Poole some years ago addressed by Sir John Jones, I was doubling as one of what he calls his "many stalkers", when he imparted a significant bit of advice that I have held on to ever since. He asked the participants a question that, in my wisdom at the time, I imagined was a trick question at best, and at worst was too complex for me to answer. See how you do...

What is the most critical role of a headteacher?
Following a pregnant pause, during which I made several notes and bullet-pointed responses, Sir John said the following, with a big smile on his face. I duly wrote it all down:

"Appointing world-class teachers, giving them a classroom, supporting and trusting them and watching the school flourish. After which you can walk around the school whistling Moon River."

I think when John talked of 'world-class teachers' here, he wasn't just referring to their technical ability, but their heart and soul and their capacity to make profound connections with every pupil, staff member and parent. Surely, these are our true 'radiators' – our true Champion Cavemen.

Sir John had supplied a brilliant answer to his question, and a straightforward one, too. When new teachers are appointed to a school, they should be seen as a gift that, if nurtured, encouraged and trusted, will achieve great things, most notably for the pupils.

The importance of supporting and trusting the teachers in our schools is crucial. Likewise, nurturing culturally aware establishments is vital if we are to create staffrooms full of contented and champion staff. This is the sentiment that sits right at the heart of our book.

Teachers enter our profession with a genuine desire to make a profound difference to the lives of the children in their care. Yet in those early years, they are so often forced back into their classrooms/caves, as schools prioritise external influences and the latest fad over the new thinking and unique expertise they have brought to their profession.

Bakers make bread, midwives deliver babies, doctors treat illness and teachers bloody teach. But they can only do this if they aren't busy doing the other things, such as compiling newsletters, preparing for a review, overseeing staff development and writing action plans and assessments, etc. While we are on the subject, when was the last time you received a newsletter from your local police force or hospital informing you of something they were introducing into their practice or providing a quarterly review of what they had achieved over the last few months? Maybe even asking for your opinion or inviting you to an open evening? I would guess that it's never. I believe that's because policing and health have a greater collective confidence in what they are doing. Perhaps these other professions are trusted and encouraged to develop and grow their moral purpose without the constant checking and force-feeding of information. Or is it that they are less accepting of external interference or the inevitable 'next thing'? I don't know.

What I do know is that staff in some schools seem to spend a lot of time living the moral purpose of others with little opportunity to articulate, reflect upon and share their own.

When this happens, we prevent staff from enjoying a sense of what is right and worthwhile, ultimately laying the groundwork for creating the Cynical Caveman of the future.

Even worse, in some schools, I fear that teachers are rarely, if ever, trusted for their ability, and they are seldom encouraged to help others learn from their experience and understanding. Staff learning comes in the form of one-way, instructional development sessions, akin to the feeding of geese on a foie gras farm.

Naturally, this may lead to a slowing down of thinking and a dulling of the teachers' creativity. Over a sustained period, it may de-energise even the keenest of staff members, as they carry around the heavy, indigestible fodder of new initiatives (see Chapter Three), which are rarely connected to their already busy lives.

We believe that if you have the right teachers on your bus, you should let them enjoy the ride and contribute to the journey. Encourage them to share their stories and practices and learn from each other. Stop occasionally to refuel, but only when you need to. Look within for inspiration, tune your own radio, set your own compass, and stop following the directions of others.

Caveman Nuggets

- Trust your staff and avoid micromanaging. It isn't worth it and could hinder development.
- In the absence of a shared vision, it can be easier to allow less significant factors to become your driving force.
- Tune your 'radio' to the frequency that meets the needs of your school community.

- Ensure you have everybody on the bus and then set the compass to *your* true north.
- 'Refuel' only when you need to.

If you have someone on the bus who isn't suited to your school's demands, your culture and your way of doing things, or they are feeling a little travel sick, pull over and let them get off. The message this delivers is of vital importance in developing confidence in what you are focusing on as a school. Why spend time involving all the staff in training and development just to compensate for a teacher who either cannot understand or does not want to follow the direction of travel?

The best way to develop responsibility in people is to give them responsibility.

Ken Blanchard – American author, business consultant and motivational speaker

Once your gang is assembled and, hopefully, even sitting in the right seats, a shared vision becomes essential for the journey ahead. This is what pulls colleagues together and helps them to articulate a collective understanding of what is possible and how and when they might achieve it.

The Vision

Your vision will become clear only when you can look into your own heart. Who looks outside, dreams; who looks inside, awakes.

Carl Jung – one of the world's most influential psychiatrists

Carl Jung's quote returns to the theme we have explored throughout this chapter (from 50 Squadron to headship). Keep looking within yourself and within your school for the answers – outside, there may only be dreams and distractions.

We believe that the inclusion of a shared vision – a school's view of what it would like to achieve and how – is essential for providing staff with focus and a clear purpose. A vision gives them the energy, motivation and possibly even the reason for getting out of bed in the morning. It is something we need to establish together to give staff a picture of the future, a glimpse of the way we want things to be, and a taste of the way they could be. Ideally, it should come from the hearts and minds of the school community it serves, free from the pollution of external pressures and a direct reflection of the effective 'groupthink' you have created as a school.

Vision is a mental picture of the future. It is an idea of what the future can hold but has not yet happened. Vision is the thing inside of us that guides us. It creates a desire to grow and improve. Vision embodies our hopes and ideals. It gives us a sense of purpose. Visions brings us flashes or glimpses of what is possible.

Chantal Bechervaise – social media influencer/blogger

A shared vision provides a plan for the school's long-term future, and when you stick to it and approach it together it gives your community direction and a mental picture of a future that is both possible and worth striving for.

Yes, at the outset, these hopes and desires may seem far into the future and intangible. Even so, just like going on a three-week road trip on the French Riviera, concluding in St. Tropez (which, at the time of writing this book, during lockdown, sounds brilliant by the way), the destination is always in focus, even though getting there takes time. Similarly, a shared vision in school becomes a reality if you place it at the school's heart and trust the staff to support it and move it forward.

It's worth noting at this point that the vision, once created, doesn't have to be set in stone. As you move through time, travelling along your collective and individual paths, it can be adjusted and renewed as the narrative and culture within the school changes. Therefore, it needs to be seen as a fluid plan rather than a static one.

> *If you don't design your own life plan, chances are you'll fall into someone else's plan. And guess what they have planned for you? Not much.*
>
> Jim Rohn – American author, entrepreneur and motivational speaker

The vision is the 'long game'; this is where you are heading, and where slow but often meaningful change can take place within a school. This is where we encourage you to invest time, energy and staff development.

However, as described throughout this book, schools are, at times, pummelled with external initiatives, which could be based on a blog doing the rounds, or even on changes to education policy. This kind of information is so relentless (and occasionally even appealing) that you may need your deflector shields at full warp to avoid being knocked off course, away from your shared vision. Of course, it's difficult not to take on board the next instruction or fad; it takes real strength to hold a steady line and not be tempted by the 'short game', especially when you are tired or looking for a ready-made solution. The history of education demonstrates that strategies may come and go but the essence of teaching remains largely unchanged. So, stand firm, invest in your shared vision and hold on tight to your beliefs.

That's not to say that, on occasion, you won't need to compromise. It could be that some of the things you are being asked to do or try, or have read, fit in with your direction of travel and could even benefit your school community and be incorporated into its vision. The key is to be discerning.

Caveman Nuggets

- Create a vision for your school involving all the staff; take your time and get this right, as it will serve as a road map for the school's future development.
- Ensure your vision is clear and accessible to all members of the school community.
- Where possible, make sure that staff development links to your vision and doesn't veer off course.

At the beginning of this chapter, I promised that we would conclude the story of Corporal Twells. Well, here goes...

It was spring 1982, and I was on holiday in Tenerife just before leaving the RAF. But on the day of my return, the UK was drawn into a conflict over the sovereignty of the Falkland Islands. As a result, on my return to base, I was informed that I would be remaining in my post for the duration of the dispute.

My role, along with the other guys of 50 Squadron, was to prepare the Vulcan bombers for a long-range bombing operation. I was tasked with setting the inertial navigation system, as the planes would be travelling with most of their navigational and radar equipment switched off to avoid detection. The others in my team worked on equally complex areas, including fitting extra fuel storage. By late April, inside a month, we were ready for Operation Black Buck, the longest bombing run in history.

Here is an extract from *History is Now* magazine, describing some of the difficulties we faced.

> *"However, there were multiple problems with this idea. The distance between Ascension Island and the Falklands was approximately 6,300 km, with the maximum effective range of the Vulcan being a mere 4,171 km. Due primarily to the plans to decommission the Vulcan that year, the aircraft had no operational air-to-air refuelling capabilities, and had not for quite some time (White, 2012). Around-the-clock engineering work was required to fix the issue and install the appropriate internal refuelling system, and to convert the aircraft's bomb bay from its current nuclear configuration back to a conventional weapons model." (Tuxford, 2016)*

Why conclude with this story? Well, I wanted to reflect on the power of togetherness and the strength derived from a group of individuals who understand their role, support each other, have a strong sense of collective direction and are trusted to achieve extraordinary things. The message of this extract and, I hope, of this chapter couldn't be more explicit – don't underestimate people's inherent ability and skill. Trust the people you employ and, with their help, find your moral purpose and direction amidst the cluttered world of education. In short, be clear about what gets you out of bed in the morning. Determine your true north.

I began this chapter with a Māori proverb that acknowledges there will be dark days. However, a team with a strong sense of moral purpose, togetherness and a shared vision can push through these challenges, leaving the shadows firmly behind.

Brighter times will always lay ahead, but the team mustn't forget how the challenges helped to strengthen and shape them.

I will leave you with a quote from Barry Masefield, who was the air electronics officer on XH 558 in 1982. This article first appeared in *The Vulcan* magazine in May 2002, as part of a special 20th Anniversary edition.

> *"What I do remember, however, is the sheer professionalism of all the aircrew and engineers involved in Black Buck, as people tackled jobs and faced situations that had never been expected, and all coped magnificently."*

Enough said.

Over to You

If you are contemplating a change in direction or introducing something new, make sure that you gather the troops around the table. Get them chatting. Get them invested. A shared vision or expectation, reached through consultation and discussion, is a powerful force. Be sure to keep checking in and reviewing your progress. If, as a group, you need to make a tweak, then agree what it is and make it. Staff autonomy will strengthen culture, build momentum and minimise confusion.

- Stick to the 'long game' (your shared vision) and be discerning when it comes to the temptation of the short game (the next bandwagon). If you are tempted, ask yourself the following questions before you introduce a new initiative to your school or at a staff meeting:

1. Does it add value to what we are currently doing?
2. Does it strengthen our shared vision? (If not, then it's probably best avoided.)

- Beware of the 'edu-pendulum'! The truth, as they say, is in the middle ground; lurching from one extreme/strategy to the other may disorientate the staff or distract them from the school's agreed direction.
- Although the benefits are irrefutable, try not to be constrained by 'evidence-informed teaching', as it may thwart staff from introducing their own creative ideas or practices. Often, the most effective teaching comes from knowing yourself and your pupils and having the courage to do what you feel is best. It might not always work, but staff flourish when there is a growing confidence and ownership in their teaching.
- Actively encourage staff to use their creativity, experience and ideas to solve problems and develop best practice across the school. Make opportunities and set the climate for staff to share their ideas, both informally and through timetabled sessions.
- Be discerning about staff development that doesn't appear to serve a useful function.

Chapter 6
The Triumvirate

Find strengths, acknowledge them, celebrate them, say thank you, repeat...

> **_Weighing the pig won't make it fatter; feeding it will._**
>
> Ian J Seath – blogger and director of Improvement Skills Consulting Ltd.

Prelude to Part I, Part II and Part III

The following chapter is split into three sections – the triumvirate – all of which explore feedback within schools in its many guises.

In the first two parts, we'll take a deeper look at monitoring and feedback, challenging our approach to some of the more well-worn events in our school calendar, namely lesson observations and the appraisal process, and providing some alternative paths of travel. Our hope is that this may move us away from the extreme negativity bias and in a more positive direction along our EduCaveman Continuum.

In the third part of the triumvirate, we uncouple feedback from monitoring, and explore how the use of regular informal feedback can be a powerful weapon in its own right, helping staff and schools along the continuum and out of the cave.

A constant theme throughout the following three sections is the different ways of finding strengths in a variety of contexts, and the importance of regularly ensuring every member of staff knows how well they are doing.

Before you read on, and in the best EduCaveman spirit, we thought we would introduce you to a word from Japanese culture – Gochisousama (pronounced go-chee-so-sah-mah). This word is used by dinner guests to express their appreciation to those who have gathered, harvested and prepared the food presented to them. In other words, guests will find your strengths, acknowledge them, celebrate them and say thank you...

The Triumvirate: Part I

Be More Dog...

In this section, we'll stress the importance of not overlooking the positives and avoiding too much focus on the negatives. To quote the Jamaican proverb, if you go to a donkey's house, don't talk about ears.

When you focus on problems you will have more problems. When you focus on possibilities then you have opportunities.

Zig Ziglar – American author and motivational speaker

OVER TO BOB...

Recently, I spent some time with old friends from my school days. We had a great get-together and plenty of time to chat. One conversation stood out above the rest. As well as making me laugh, it resonated with me, as it was so relevant to this chapter and had me scrambling for a notebook and pen to write it down.

My old mate Seamus was talking about his love of dogs and how much he enjoyed being in their company. I jokingly said, "You seem to love your dogs more than your family." He looked me in the eye and replied, "Of course I do, they mean the world to me."

Knowing I had dogs, he continued by saying, "Look, suppose you were to accidentally lock your partner and dog in the garage. You then go out for a few drinks and a spot of lunch with your friends and return some five hours later a little worse for wear. What do you think would be the outcome?"

(Should you ever find yourself in this scenario, our strong recommendation would be to contact Relate immediately!)

Before I got the chance to answer, he added, "Let me help you. On your return, you walk down the drive and become aware of your error when you hear screaming and shouting and a little barking and scratching (which you hope is the dog) from your garage. Your heart sinks and you have a sick feeling (plus the hope you didn't leave the hammer accessible) as you head to free your accidental hostages.

"What do you think will happen when your victims are freed? Yes, you guessed right. Your partner will go beyond ballistic, calling you all the names under the sun, including the old favourites that normally crop up at these moments: "You're useless", "You never think of me", "Why didn't you answer your phone?", "Did it not occur to that tiny brain of yours what you had done?" The atmosphere for the rest of the evening will be cool to borderline permafrost, and thawing will take you well beyond the next UN climate change talks!

"Meanwhile, your other victim, the dog, will greet you with her tail wagging while barking loudly and trying desperately to give you a big lick. This will continue for the next few minutes as she contorts her body in an S-like motion, wanting to show you affection. When you settle down to watch television later that evening, she will nuzzle up to you on the sofa after realising you have been put into forced isolation in your own home."

I found Seamus's tale quite thought-provoking. Both victims love you; one married you and helped you to raise a family, the other you purchased as a puppy (or rescued) and took home to become part of your family. However, their responses couldn't be more different.

You see, your partner is like most people (myself included) and hardwired to find fault – the old negativity bias at work again. In this situation, they quickly lose sight of your strengths, the core reasons they have stuck with you for the last twenty years: you're great with the kids, you make them laugh, you're sensitive and you're always honest and kind, etc. But because of your blunder, their brain filters out your many strengths and focuses on the error, which leads them to think you're stupid, forgetful and are always out with your mates.

What receives attention or focus becomes what we (or the client) strive(s) for and eventually becomes a reality.

Erika Stoerkel – coach and author

The dog, however, loves you unconditionally and, despite being held captive for the same five hours, focuses only on your strengths. She is incapable of seeing anything other than the best in you; her love shines through. After all, you feed her, show her lots of affection, take her for great walks, give her treats and even pick up her poo! Therefore, on your return, she is as happy as Larry to see you. In her mind, there is no need to remind you of your silly, small error. Dogs seem to be hardwired to value and trust those around them. They see the best in you always.

Caveman Consideration

- Try not to let negative thoughts dominate your relationship with others. Instead, focus on strengths and build that relationship, even when you can see weaknesses in front of you.

- Start training yourself. Can you acquire more comfort with losing the battle but winning the war? In this context, 'the war' is helping to nurture more confident and competent colleagues, whilst developing a professional relationship that is brimming with trust.

- Keep your eye on the prize and be careful not to pick holes. Come on – just *be more dog*.

I reflected on this story for a while and began to see its relevance as a wonderful lead into the triumvirate, where we explore the ease with which school life and systems can, on occasion, make us feel cautious and push us firmly onto the back foot. This establishes a default setting in us to focus on the negative and see the worst in situations and sometimes, sadly, in others, too. It is balanced throughout the sub-chapters with our key message about the joy of finding strengths in others, acknowledging their contributions, celebrating their success and remembering to say thank you – the very thrust of our tale above.

Before we move on, we invite you to take a moment to picture what would happen if we were to refocus the energy and mindset we currently apply to seeking out what *isn't* working in schools towards finding out what *is* working... imagine that!

Where did/do we learn to focus on the negative?

The 'Lesson Observation'

For most teachers, the negative trail starts right back in training, with those first observations and follow-up target-setting meetings. It's a system that continues through our early teaching years, and far beyond.

From the outset, we are taught and encouraged to focus on what isn't working well. We are then set targets relating to those perceived 'weaknesses', and our progress is measured against them. "System established, system maintained – full steam ahead, Captain."

Even worse, as soon as you had completed the first observation as a trainee or teacher, then guess what? Yep, it was followed by the next observation. This continues time after time throughout your career. After all, it is a tried and tested method, and one I feel sure has been used since the beginning of early civilisation (rinse and repeat ad infinitum).

However, after every observation, you re-enter the next part of the fray at a bit of a disadvantage, as this time you don't have a clean sheet, or a clean bill of health – you have already been well and truly rumbled and, in some cases, you are on the ropes and breathing hard. 'They' and others in the know (usually the leadership team) already have a good idea that you are proficient in some areas and bloody ordinary – borderline weak – in others. It's printed on a sheet in front of them. And so, the cycle continues.

Once 'they' have the information, it can put you in defensive mode whenever they enter the room, especially if it is to carry out another observation. And, no matter how hard you try during the follow-up observed lessons to demonstrate that you are calm and looking forward to the experience, having taken on board the feedback from the previous lesson, you will be rumbled. If anything goes slightly wrong, or they start talking to Darren or Summer, even though you have put them strategically in seats difficult to access by any human not wearing crampons, you forget to smile, you forget to enjoy the experience and can even become defensive and anxious. Worse still, you can start to feel powerless and a little out of control. We know, we have been there!

During these observations (the event), I sometimes sweated more than an arsonist in a firework shop on Bonfire Night. Unsurprisingly, I was just not relaxed and the whole experience was far from enjoyable (recognise anything here?).

This anxiety can be heightened yet further if the build-up to the big day is over a period of weeks and written in stone in the diary. If only it was a curry night at Wetherspoons with friends and family, or a pedicure at Clarins, but this is the head and the maths lead, suited and booted, checking you out from the back of the room with a clipboard in hand. By the time the dreaded date arrives, you have already overanalysed the lesson so much that you are well below par when the enemy enters.

Even so, by the end of any observed lesson, you have usually demonstrated some progress against the previously agreed targets. "YES!" We are teachers after all! However, this can often be quickly overlooked with little recognition or admiration for your achievement. Instead, as a perverse way of saying "well done," you'll be given two new targets – two new areas of weakness you didn't even know you had that morning. Yet these have suddenly become the highlight of the discussion, the new message of improvement. Unbelievable!

Caveman Nuggets

Be the one who points out what is going right and helps when things are going wrong.

The journey home heralded new horizons. You now have two new targets: two new bits of negative baggage on the back seat to dwell on until next time – arrgghh! Of course, good things probably were mentioned, as they generally are, but in my case, just as I am sure it is with many others, I only focused on the negative, sometimes for days on end. The things I was doing wrong went round and round in my head like a tumble dryer with a broken timer.

Even worse is the feedback that can arrive days, even a week, later – yes it can happen – leaving you in a state of anxiety and apprehension in the interim. I think this approach should be outlawed under a 'Cruelty to Teachers Act'. It often leads to high levels of anxiety and a teacher who will certainly not be able to tune into the positive stuff.

Caveman Nuggets

It's easy to become preoccupied with even-better-ifs, next steps and talking about targets that haven't been met; these things come naturally to us. Let us resist this time-worn path and ensure any feedback we provide is balanced by what is going well with staff and building on their strengths.

Can you start meetings by sharing effective practice, either yours or a colleague's?

Sadly, as we are promoted to a position where we carry out observations as the 'expert', we perpetuate this approach with ease – entering classrooms like a sheriff, a clipboard resting easily on our hip.

We don't do this because we want some form of revenge (although it might feel like that to the person being observed) but because throughout our teaching career, we have learned to focus and rely on a deficit model. We have been looking for the problems for too long and this has become our reality. We just can't help ourselves; it's how we do things.

Maybe we need to hit the refresh button, ditch the termly or bi-annual formal lesson observation approach altogether and replace it with a more informal, regular process with lower stakes. This would focus less on judgement and more on development.

Rather than 'lesson observations' per se, headteachers and/ or other leaders could continue their classroom visits if they wanted to, but the aim of them would be more in keeping with our message in Chapter Four, in which we urged Champion Cavemen to wear out their shoe leather to strengthen relationships.

What's more, these visits could also provide an opportunity to give regular informal positive feedback (see Part III of this chapter) which, as we know, can work wonders for both confidence and morale.

Finally, they could serve as a useful tool for the headteacher or other leaders to take the temperature of the school, securing an overall picture of teaching and learning. This would naturally lead to the sharing of effective practice whilst identifying general trends that could be addressed through a combination of one-to-one sessions and development involving the entire staff. Using this approach could provide greater opportunity to share strengths and talk about teaching and learning on a more regular basis.

At the heart of this process is the development of the staff; it's not one that is driven by the need to be accountable to external visitors. It's a simple, no-fuss approach that will give a clearer, more current and more honest picture of what is happening in the school. Farewell to the one-off performing monkey!

This system is all well and good, but supposing it revealed an aspect of practice that couldn't be chatted through or addressed over a coffee? Well, if the visitor, whilst walking the patch, thought a teacher required more development, this could take the form of a coaching session. The coaching session might well involve the visitor (coach) working alongside the teacher (coachee) to reach an agreed understanding of the classroom's current reality (see Chapter Eight). The coach would achieve this through skillful and planned questioning, which would enable the teacher to identify what changes they wanted to target in their practice, and how they would go about that process – their strategies, in other words.

This presupposes that the coachee already has the solutions within them but has not yet joined the dots. The coach is not acting as an expert in this situation but comes to the conversation offering a service. They are acting as an equal partner, a sounding board or mirror for the teacher to share their perceptions and articulate their own solutions. The process, if effective, will leave the coachee feeling empowered, energised and motivated to develop an aspect of their practice that they have self-identified.

Another approach on the coaching continuum is the use of 'instructional coaching'. This is when the coach acts as an expert, identifying possible targets from the outset and the strategies or small steps that the teacher will need to take to achieve their goal. However, unlike the traditional approach to lesson observations mentioned earlier in the chapter, the instructional coach will take full responsibility for helping the teacher to practise and learn new strategies through modelling, observation of others and direct feedback. The connection between the observer (instructional coach) and the teacher is regular, builds trust in the system and supports the individual's development.

These two coaching approaches, and the low-stakes regular visits, are far removed from the more traditional lesson observation approach. The observer is no longer responsible for creating a list of things to do (targets), which they then hand over to the teacher to complete with little support or guidance. Our alternative identifies what is going well and what needs attention, offering a menu of tailored development when required.

Just to be clear, we are not suggesting that coaching should only occur when there is a problem. Coaching and opportunities for collegiate working should take place even when teaching and learning are strong. If we can nurture a low-stakes culture, where the discussion and development of teaching and learning sits right at the core of what we do, then surely we'll be on the right path.

Caveman Consideration

- Stop treating observations as a diarised event, an opportunity to gather data under surveillance or as an overview for a report.

- If appropriate, change the mindset in the school. Start seeing observations as a developmental process rather than a judgemental one. This is a process in which practice should be observed throughout the year, during many different drop-ins, and these observations should form the basis of an ongoing discussion. They should involve a learning process for both participants,

> providing a genuine opportunity to discuss practice and approaches in an open, less threatening way.
>
> - Take a serious look at the benefits of coaching (see Chapter Seven) and then coach, coach, coach!
> - Buddy up staff with differing strengths so they can share their expertise. Learn from each other, whether you are carrying out drop-ins, observing or co-teaching.
> - When considering development points, ensure you give strengths the same weight.

Staff using this approach will be more relaxed, as the staged event no longer exists, and they can approach discussions surrounding practice on a more even footing. They will also be more receptive to feedback, particularly when it's positive, as they are having regular discussions about learning, have confidence in the system and the trust account is high.

As we conclude this section, please remember that teaching and learning are deeply personal. We give them our all and, consequently, separating the personal from the professional during feedback can be challenging – to say the least. With this in mind, we simply ask you to explore further opportunities to *be more dog*. Where you can, find strengths, celebrate them, acknowledge them, say thank you, repeat...

Over to You

Given the cultural importance of this chapter's content, we make no apology for the length of this section. It's our hope that many of our ideas will resonate with you. It would be reassuring to think that in our professional interactions, we could leave colleagues in a better place than when we found them. Good business is when both parties leave the table happy, and while education certainly isn't business, I think the sentiment holds. We'd all like to think that the person we've been working with left the experience feeling confident, empowered and motivated to change and that we will feel privileged in knowing that we had a hand in this.

We also hope that this chapter has whet your appetite in relation to the different ways in which you can support colleagues to achieve their best; whether that's through an opportunity that has arisen whilst wearing out your shoe leather or through coaching or instructional coaching. Whatever process is used, you will almost certainly be providing feedback.

So, here's the good news: feedback really can make all the difference. Now for the bad news: feedback really can make all the difference! With this in mind, it's worth taking the time to get it right. The most important thing to remember with feedback is that it's not about what you *say*, it's about what they *hear*.

Caveman groundwork...

So, before diving in, let's do the necessary preparation to maximise our impact. The following questions may be worth mulling over to ensure a positive outcome while working with a fellow caveman:

- Do they trust me? What can I do to build up the trust account? (See Chapter Nine)

- Do they respect me professionally? If the answer isn't clear, what actions can I take to ensure the respect is there? Perhaps they could come and watch me teach? Could we team-teach?

- When was the last time I gave this person feedback? Was it last year, as part of their annual appraisal, or was it last week, as part of the informal feedback I regularly provide? If it was the latter, there shouldn't be any surprises and any developmental points will be easy to agree given the trusting relationship that has been established through regular working practice. If it's the former, what actions can I take to ensure a healthy culture of regular informal feedback? (See Part III of this chapter.)

- What are my motives? If my aim is to raise awareness and support development, I'm on the right track. Conversely, if I am using this as an opportunity to prove that I am right, for one-upmanship or to punish, blame or get personal, then I need to rethink. My focus should be on performance, not personality, and I should only proceed if I have good intentions.

- Have I asked them when and where would be a good time to meet/work together? Whilst the time and place may be convenient for me, it might not be for them...

- Feedback is most effective when it takes place as close to the event as possible. If for any reason I can't meet with the person I've been working with, what holding actions can I take? If you are watching a colleague teach, ensure that you don't leave them hanging. The last thing they want is the anxiety of wondering what you think. It's important that you manage this.

The execution

Just before you meet a colleague, bear in mind the following points:

- Adopt a developmental mindset rather than a judgmental one. Take a stance of curiosity. Being accusatory may elicit a defensive response.
- Be non-judgemental. Try and be descriptive rather than evaluative – be a mirror. You can rely on facts, but interpretations are debatable. Compare, "The behaviour of your pupils was shocking today" with, "I noticed that Jill, Jenny and John talked over you today."
- Be specific, not general.
- Avoid using the language of absolutes – always, never, all, etc. This may provoke a defensive reaction. In my experience, the more accurate you can be with your comments, the less resistance you will encounter.
- Ensure that the process is participatory or dialogic. Invite discussion.

- Avoid giving mixed messages. If you are nervous about discussing a developmental point, ensure that you guard against providing a raft of positives to soften the blow. This approach may dilute the one developmental point that needs to be discussed.

- Don't give more than a couple of developmental points. Preferably, these actions will have already been identified by the person you're working with (see Chapter Eight). If they can't self-identify, encourage clarity through questions like, "Tell me about today?"

- Lose the battle but win the war. Here, the war is helping to nurture more empowered, confident and competent teachers whilst developing a professional relationship that is brimming with trust. The battle is informing them that a display border tape is flapping. Keep your eye on the prize and be careful not to pick holes. Let's be clear: I'm not advocating that we drop our expectations, I am simply suggesting that we remain focused on the 'long game' of Champion Caveman Culture. During feedback, will the identification of the loose border tape on the display help the 'long game'? Hmm...

- Let me be even more controversial. If there aren't any next steps, don't create them. Let the member of staff bask in their glory. Just ensure (through focusing on cause and effect) that they are entirely clear about how their exemplary practice ensured first-class outcomes for the learners and finish there. A possible next step, if you really want one, is to explore how they can share their practice with colleagues.

- If appropriate, use feedback as an opportunity to administer confidence first aid. If a team member has been going through a tough time and is still performing well, give them what they need – a boost.

- Try to avoid unsolicited advice, as this can disempower and create dependency (see Chapter Eight). Unhelpful phrases include, "If I were you, I would have…", "What you should have done is…" and "I wouldn't have done that."

Whilst feeding back, try and remember the following points:

- It's an obvious one, but remember to say thank you for the opportunity to work with them.

- Get off to a positive start and encourage interaction and ownership of the process. For example, if you have just watched a colleague teach, you might ask them, "What was the best five minutes of your lesson?" or "What were you most proud of today?" If you agree, make sure you affirm their thoughts. If the teaching and learning were superb, keep asking, "What else?"

- You might also ask them for the five factors that had the biggest positive impact on learning. If this comes easily, why not ask them for a further five? Can you overdo the positives with teachers? – no! The more the better, especially when considering the extreme negativity bias (see Chapter Two). Cavemen staff typically need to practise articulating what they do well. They may find this difficult and may squirm, but make sure you persist – they'll thank you for it in the long run, even if it doesn't seem like it at the time.

Remind them that this isn't boasting. Don't brush over effective practice – help them to break it down and be clear about the cause and effect.

- If you are asked for advice, try providing several suggestions or options. This will ensure your colleague retains an element of ownership. When doing this, help them to focus on the future, as they can't change what has gone before. Try saying things like, "OK, perhaps next lesson you could try…" or "You could have a go at… Let me know how it goes."

- Ask for feedback on your feedback! If the session hasn't been helpful, can you reach a shared agreement on what the next session might look like? A healthy feedback culture goes up, down and sideways.

Health warning

I'm stating the obvious here, but remember that providing positive feedback publicly is fine, but shaming people in public isn't. Where you can, provide developmental feedback in person, one to one. And just to be clear, by in person, I don't mean sending an email. Providing developmental feedback this way is less than ideal because:

a.) Neither the sender nor the receiver can read body language.

b.) It negates the extent to which the process is dialogic/interactive.

c.) The sender can't guarantee that it has been read.

And finally, only provide feedback on behaviours that can be changed. Accents, for example, cannot be altered. Asking someone to address their whiney voice might not end well!

The Triumvirate: Part II

Waiting for Godot

In this part of Chapter Six, we'll explore the traditional school appraisal process and how it links to our Caveman Continuum.

Don't lower your expectations to meet your performance.
Raise your level of performance to meet your expectations.

Ralph Marston – American author and founder of *The Daily Motivator*, which can be found at www.greatday.com

 **OVER TO BOB...**

Empurrar com a barriga

Literal meaning: *To push something with your belly.*
Alternative meaning: *To keep postponing an important chore.*

You may wonder why we are linking the Portuguese idiom above with the appraisal process. The reason is that, unfortunately, we still come across appraisals that are akin to pushing something with your belly. They are slow, laborious, often inappropriate to the setting and strung out over long periods. Therefore, they are often readily postponed in favour of something – make that anything – that is deemed more urgent, more in need of attention and possibly even more appealing. You see, the act of carrying out and completing appraisals in some settings is not engaging for the recipient or the appraiser. While it's good to get them ticked off the list, they're rarely an effective tool for improvement, and so other, more important things are allowed to get in the way. In some schools, it may be yet another 'mind in neutral' exercise amid the busy annual cycle of things to complete.

> *Performance management is not about complicated procedures, piles of paperwork or adding to teachers' and leaders' already overburdened workload. It's about recording the great practice, reflecting on progress, and – this is the key – developing your staff (and thereby your children) to be the best they can be. After all, isn't that what education is all about?*
>
> Betsy Maytham – experienced teacher and trainer

However, we equally come across schools that use appraisal as a hugely effective tool in their armoury. The resulting impact on individual performance ultimately leads to school development and a strengthening of the culture. They achieve this through a structured, rigorous process that has regular and sustained focus, feedback and coaching at its heart. Add appropriate targeted training and development opportunities into the mix and you're onto a winner. We'll discuss these added ingredients in more detail later in the book.

In appraisals that are not so effective, we usually find the model has become more important than the process. In these schools, the focus is on accountability, with less emphasis on development. The evidence is logged on formatted sheets and filed along with years of previous evidence before being locked away in a cupboard marked the *Never Never Land* in the Lost Boys section. The file comes with clear instructions not to be opened until the following year's appraisal is done – terminé. Open Pandora's Box at your peril!

The journey usually begins with a target-setting meeting. This is generally in September, but it's a movable feast and can easily drift into the second half-term if other things have become 'more important'.

The targets set are annual overarching goals, usually two or three in number, that are 'negotiated' in the preliminary discussions, and so it begins...

I say discussions, but in many cases, the targets are partially set (semifreddo) well before the meeting takes place and well before a word has even been uttered between you. This can leave you with the distinct impression that the appraiser is either a part-time mind reader, a full-time psychic or a member of The Magic Circle, who has conjured up these targets from your subconscious.

While potentially true in some schools (if you are lucky!), it is far from the truth in most. The reality is, your appraiser, and others who form the appraisal team, will be aware of the school priorities that they will need to work on over the coming year. As a result, they have usually created the targets well in advance of the meeting to distribute the huge workload. This makes the target-setting meeting's purpose almost redundant, leaving its only aim seemingly to persuade – maybe even coerce – you into believing that your agreed final targets have been created by you and your appraiser. Though perhaps that last bit is a little too cynical and exposes my deep-down opinion of this approach!

The time between the first target-setting meeting at the start of September and the target-review meeting at the end of the year can be ten school months (just two months shy of the average lifespan of a house mouse!). The end-of-year review meeting is a kind of rounding up, a completion of the cycle. During this plenary discussion, should you get through the meeting reasonably quickly and are not too weary from the summer term's demands, there may be time to move swiftly onto next year's cycle. You might also be able to set your targets for next year. Bingo – job done – tick!

During the ten months between the two meetings, you are pretty much safe in assuming that not one discussion will be had, or any feedback provided, relating to how you are doing and how you might progress further towards the negotiated targets that were set. It is as though you have shared a secret and have promised never to discuss it – the school equivalent of a verbal lockdown. Your progress, or lack of it, will be explained to you at the end of the process, when the school year has ended. (Not too long to wait if you are patient!) At this endpoint in the appraisal cycle, you will need to gather evidence to demonstrate what you have achieved and the progress you have made against your set targets over the previous ten months. Good luck with remembering any of the details, as personally, I always struggled at this point.

It is easy to see why this approach may not be seen as an effective way of helping staff to develop – it's not rocket science. When asked, most staff want to know they are doing well, and they want this feedback regularly – ideally, daily. They certainly don't want it once or twice a year.

> **It is important to avoid waiting until judgement day when working on strengthening your performance management system.**
>
> Margaret Graziano – one of Silicon Valley's Top 100 Influential Women in Business and the CEO and founder of KeenAlignment

Having described an appraisal model that seems so ineffective, you could be forgiven for assuming it's an historic format used shortly after quills were introduced into the classroom. Sadly, this isn't the case. I'd wager that this kind of model is still found in schools up and down the country, where it continues to suck the life out of staff on both sides of the fence, fortunately only on an annual basis.

Hopefully, you can now see the link with the chapter title. If not, let me assist. In the play *Waiting for Godot* by Samuel Beckett, time for the two main characters, Vladimir and Estragon, moves slowly and meaninglessly in cycles. They are patiently awaiting the arrival of the mysterious Godot (the appraiser), who sends word of his imminent arrival but never actually appears... Sound familiar? Another cancelled meeting? After much soul searching and discussion of their existence, Vladimir and Estragon decide their lives have meaning and there is a reason for their being, and that Godot, when he eventually arrives, will help them make this clearer. Can you see the link now?

Caveman Nuggets

Checking in not *checking up.*

At this stage, you are probably wondering why I seem such an expert on this flawed approach. Well, the answer is easy: it was the very one that Dave and I used with aplomb. It seemed a perfectly tailored way to 'tick off' another task on the annual cycle of things to complete. We fell into the trap early on as headteachers. That said, we were neither lazy nor disinterested, and we're certainly not aiming those labels at schools who might work this way now. Within the fullness of the days, it was, and possibly still is, difficult to envisage a new system. After all, it seemed to work, didn't it?

Thankfully, schools have been cracking the mould for some time now, creating or refreshing the appraisal system to produce more effective solutions to staff development. This leads to a more sustainable, more fulfilled approach to school development that is enjoyed and trusted by one and all. It's one that puts individual learning, not justification, at the heart of the process.

Key to the more successful of these processes is regular ongoing dialogue to identify progress towards agreed goals and targets. This focuses and builds on individual strengths, providing a clear structure that gives the participants the time and permission to think through and discuss practice on a regular basis.

In schools that are using appraisal more effectively, the system is alive and kicking and sewn into the fabric. It is very much part of the culture, and everybody enjoys its immediacy, as it supports and guides staff to develop throughout the year. It is visible to everyone and referred to constantly through regular informal and formal discussions and short drop-ins (see Part I of this chapter). The biannual, judgemental event where you are summoned to explain yourself is avoided at all costs.

Within a revised system, regular feedback and coaching highlight the things that are going well. Staff are comfortable with discussing and sharing progress and hearing good things. Indeed, they are actively encouraged to do the right thing (develop) because they understand what good looks like, as it is described and discussed as part of the appraisal. The constant focus on things that are not going well is replaced with supporting and guiding participants towards professional growth. This unashamedly builds on their strengths, reinforcing what needs to continue well before the focus turns towards fixing any identified weaknesses or deficits. In short, it removes the need to prove oneself.

This approach does not mean the system forgoes rigour or consideration about agreed areas for development and progress. It doesn't. If it is to be respected and successful, it must be structured and understood by everyone. It also needs to be conducted within the framework of the school's vision, targets and aims, otherwise it could become overwhelming and things could easily get out of control, adding unnecessary focus and work to already busy schools.

When using this approach to appraisal, the system doesn't feel like it is being done to you, but rather alongside you, which is more encouraging and useful. Discussion and coaching throughout the year centres on developing staff practice, with the agreed emphasis on personal learning and growth rather than performance. This will benefit staff enormously and, ultimately, have a positive impact on school development.

When an effective appraisal system successfully becomes part of the school culture, trust levels greatly improve because of the change in emphasis already described. The staff will be far more receptive and open, and ready to receive information about the kind of things they can work on together to develop their teaching, their role and the school community. It becomes a significant part of a school's ability to inspire and engage staff to move their practice forward and, ultimately, it creates stronger engagement in the school's shared vision. It becomes a win-win process to be enjoyed and looked forward to.

A key point here is that performance management is a continuous process – not a once-a-year activity. Quality performance management should, therefore, bring together a number of different, integrated activities to form an ongoing performance management cycle.

Taken from an article on ClearReview.com – a continuous performance management software company

Many appraisal systems exist across our schools, including the highly effective ones described here. Whatever approach you decide on, or choose to tweak, amend or maintain, it will only be valid if it is meaningful to the appraisee and to the school.

We suggest that learning and development, through regular coaching and feedback, should be prioritised over the need for staff to prove their progress against a long-forgotten set of targets. We go further and assert that it must also ensure staff ownership in the process, especially at the outset when targets are being discussed and set.

Our sincere hope is that this chapter has given you the time to reflect more deeply on the effectiveness of your current appraisal system, enabling you to move your thinking forward and ensure that your team are not pushing this process with their bellies…

Over to You

If, after reading this chapter, you are feeling slightly uneasy about your current appraisal system, perhaps the following questions will help move your thinking on, and, in turn, help you and your team move closer to a more meaningful process.

Does your current appraisal process allow for regular informal and formal:

- Discussions about effective teaching and learning?
- Communication?
- Collaboration (meetings between both parties and other colleagues)?
- Discussions about progress (rather than targets)?
- Discussions about how to build on strengths (not just developmental areas)?
- Discussions about opportunities for development?

Does your current appraisal process make a difference? If yes, to whom and how?

Progress and improvements are not state secrets that can only be revealed to the appraisee at the end of the year in a darkened, quiet room, having been led there blindfolded.

Our message is simple: be open, transparent and gear your system to focus on driving staff development.

Once your new system is up and running, the chances are there will be an abundance of opportunities to work with one another as you explore and develop different aspects of teaching and learning. Don't forget to have another look at the information and suggestions we provided at the end of Part I. We hope they will support the process of coaching and feedback and maximise the impact of your work together.

The Triumvirate: Part III

Silence Isn't Golden...

In this section, we'll uncouple feedback from monitoring and explore how the use of regular informal feedback can be a powerful weapon in its own right.

The most powerful drug in the world is kindness. It works for everyone, it's very hard to get the dose wrong and it's free at the point of delivery.

Dr Phil Hammond – broadcaster, physician, comedian and commentator on health issues

 OVER TO BOB...

Avere gli occhi foderati di prosciutto

This Italian saying means not seeing or understanding the obvious; you are literally unable to see what is directly in front of you because your eyes are lined with ham! In this chapter, the third and final part of the triumvirate, we will steer you away from this blindness and pull the pork from your eyes (excuse the expression), encouraging you to explore other ways of developing school culture through the provision of more effective feedback.

As educators, when we think about monitoring and feedback, the first thing that comes to mind is often the lesson observation. This is a school staple used in many educational settings worldwide, and it's something we explored in detail in the first part of this chapter. However, beyond this process, school life is packed with the give and take of feedback, much of which contributes to the staff feeling more positive and energised (though some of it has less of an effect).

One of the most powerful forms of feedback for highlighting staff strengths and giving a positive message is informal feedback. This kind of feedback can be given during brief interactions as staff move around the school sharing time together – hence the importance of wearing out your shoe leather, which we explored in detail in Chapter Four.

- *69% of employees said they would work harder if they felt their efforts were better recognised.*
- *Four out of ten workers are actively disengaged when they get little or no feedback.*

- ***39% of employees reported that they don't feel appreciated at work.***

  Information taken from 11 Eye-Opening Statistics on the Importance of Employee Feedback (an infographic).

  Lindsay Kolowich Cox – blogger and creator of educational content for marketers

Although snatched in a moment and rarely planned, this kind of feedback is so often affirmative; we would, therefore, advocate that you plan intentional walkabouts to tell staff the 'good stuff'. It is irrelevant whether this praise is given by a peer or someone in a leadership role. It confirms to the recipient the good things they are doing. For example, "Loved the assembly", "The choir sang beautifully" or "Thanks for all your planning ideas the other evening." You get the picture. If delivered sincerely, how can this feedback not lead to happier, more positive staff and encourage stronger relationships across the school? After all, as we will go on to mention later, in The Intermission, it is the very glue that binds a school community together.

There are two things people want more than sex and money – recognition and praise.

Mary Kay Ash – American businesswoman who founded Mary Kay Cosmetics

When it occurs regularly, informal feedback is potent and transformational. This is because it lifts our spirits, motivates us and makes us feel good. Why wouldn't it? It also helps us to understand and clarify our strengths, giving us licence to do more of the same. In effect, we are spreading a little kindness around the school and creating and/or modelling a culture through these actions, ensuring staff are more likely to go the extra mile for the pupils, the school and its community.

Ultimately, if an individual feels good about themselves, and more emotionally connected to the school and its culture, they are more likely to do more of the same and even exceed what is required of them. They will become intrinsically motivated to go beyond their job description – discretionary effort in action (more on that later, in The Intermission). This will then impact their team's performance, and any goodwill generated will permeate the school community's culture. Easy really!

Caveman Considerations

- Remember to say thank you; everyone likes to be thanked.

- Encourage and model informal feedback as part of your school's culture. Recognise staff for their contributions and start spreading the good news. There is plenty of it around – you just need to tune in. This process is not reserved for those in leadership; anyone can do it – you don't need permission.

- Plan deliberate time slots in which to have regular positive conversations with colleagues in your team or school. This has nothing to do with the appraisal process or targets; it is just an enjoyable chat about your practice, progress and how this can be best supported. Imagine if every member of your school had this wonderful opportunity as a given – a cultural expectation.

- When you have some down time (it does happen occasionally!) treat yourself and your colleagues to a walk around the school. Make connections, chat and give some informal feedback and praise.
- Encourage your colleagues to be cultural attachés (aka Champion Cavemen) and insist on the positive acknowledgement of all staff, by all staff, ideally on a daily basis.
- Whoever you are, when you are walking around the school and wearing out your shoe leather, recognise the contributions of everybody. They will love it!
- As a school leader, why not timetable a staff meeting each month to involve a walk around the school, with a coffee in hand, to spend time in classrooms sharing the good stuff?
- Some of your colleagues will find it hard to hear or receive positive feedback. In fact, they simply won't believe it or will play it down. Don't let this stop you! Often, it is these colleagues who need to hear it the most.

Silent praise

Giving positive feedback to colleagues is such a simple thing to do, and yet it is so often neglected. Why? We have a theory about this that we call silent praise; an unconscious phenomenon that is happening in schools across the land. Typically, silent praise happens when staff walk around the school with their praise firmly locked in their heads (or the ham metaphorically resting over their eyes). They know you are a great teacher, and they know you worked incredibly hard last week setting up the online parents' evening, but it would seem they just don't know how to acknowledge this and say thank you. They think that you will somehow pick up this praise via telepathy as they smile at you knowingly during the walkabout. They believe their mere presence is saying all they need to say. Consequently, your inner voice provides you with the all-too-familiar reassurance of, "I must be doing OK as no one has told me otherwise." I'm sure you'll agree that in these circumstances, silence is certainly not golden.

Let's knock that myth on the head immediately. We know that staff need to hear the good stuff, and regularly. Imagine going through life with your partner without ever shining a light on the joy you gain from being with them, assuming that because you are thinking it, this will be enough. I am not a counsellor, but I can assure you that this will lead to problems from the outset. Your relationship will undoubtedly be tested. If you don't believe me, try silent praise for a week at home and let us know the outcome at #YoureWonderfulButSorryIDidntTellYou.

Now think of the lovely staff in your department or throughout the whole school, who may go a week, or even a term, without any informal positive feedback or praise. Yes, this can happen. Imagine how they feel as they drive home. Check it out at #WhyDoIBotherNobodyReallyCares.

Silent gratitude isn't much use to anyone.
Gertrude Stein – novelist, playwright, poet and avid art collector

So, if you are one of those people who find this approach difficult, then start practising. Find some time to get out and pass on the praise. (We suggest you avoid giving it randomly to passing pedestrians but instead focus on your team!) If you feel awkward, remember that you're probably not alone, especially if you are not the gushy type. Giving praise and positive feedback doesn't always come easily to people, especially in the busy world of schools and classrooms. In this situation, you may have to adapt your style, because others may be reliant on feedback and someone being effusive about their practice. So, 'fake it till you make it' and one day you'll genuinely feel it. After all, we are teachers, and most of us have at least one Oscar nomination in the Best Actor/Actress category for some of our performances!

However, you will need to bear in mind that it takes time to change engrained habits and develop completely new ones. Remember that they are not events but processes. As such, you may falter occasionally. As long as your focus remains on the desired change, this won't matter. Trust me, the more you do it, the easier it becomes.

We are acutely aware that our suggestions may be a bridge too far for our Cynical Caveman, simply because he is exhausted and malnourished. His reservoirs of hope and positivity have all but run dry and may even have left the building. Any remaining energy is being fully utilised to keep him upright and thus can't be expended on giving you the positive feedback you need. However, if you feel pessimistic, tired and cynical, we encourage you to try and summon the energy to feed back something positive, as the very act of giving it will nourish you. What goes around comes around, so why not give it a whirl?

Caveman Consideration

- Work together to create a culture that makes positive praise and recognition commonplace and part of the fabric of your school. Whilst we acknowledge that school leaders play an enormous part in setting the tone and creating this kind of culture, it needs and takes every member of staff to maintain it and make it part of the norm.

- If your colleagues aren't wearing out their shoe leather and are a little reluctant, then be the first and set an example. Get the ball rolling and others should soon follow. And remember to nourish your first followers. (Look up "The Dancing Guy" clip on YouTube.)

- Every member of staff needs to experience the power and benefit of regular informal feedback, especially leaders and office staff, who often receive few comments on their work, save from irate parents or frustrated children. As a headteacher, I rarely received informal feedback. I often look back with fondness at my time with an old colleague, who I nicknamed the Angel of the South – Mary D. She would regularly knock on my door and pass on a positive message about something I had done around the school. I can't tell you how elated her comments made me feel. If your line manager is doing an excellent job, find the time to tell them; you'll make their day, and that comment may carry them for weeks or even months.

- Avoid silent praise as a means of passing on a message. It won't get through unless the person knows how to read minds or is part of The Magic Circle!

- If you struggle to give praise to colleagues, and you are not the effusive type, then practise. 'Fake it till you make it' and one day you might genuinely feel it.

Formal feedback in schools, unlike informal feedback, often takes place in a planned and systematic way, through the appraisal process, teaching and learning observations and external visits, etc. It is usually an event, something that you are invited to be part of, though often not as an equal partner.

During this type of feedback, the recipients will often find it difficult to listen actively and may become distracted from the conversation's thrust; usually because they are on the back foot and fear the worst (our Cautious Caveman). This feeling is akin to when you were ten years old and were called downstairs for a dressing-down from your parents.

The recipients in these situations are rarely in ready-to-receive mode (remember our Congested Caveman in Chapter Three?), because they instinctively anticipate the direction of travel the feedback will take. They perceive the process will be one way – a monologue, if you like – and will offer little, if any, encouragement for them to contribute. It is done to them not with them.

This has been so clearly demonstrated in the many Ofsted feedback meetings I have attended. Ask any attendee to cite the salient strengths that were outlined in the meeting and they may remember some of them. However, ask them to recount the key weaknesses and they will reel them off verbatim. In this kind of scenario, we are experts at identifying what went wrong and confirming our worst nightmares. As stated previously, we are not conditioned to recognise what is going well. Hence, we become defensive and deaf to the good noise – the extreme negativity bias in action.

This reaction is probably because formal feedback in schools is synonymous with judgement rather than staff development. This isn't hugely surprising given the years of high-stakes accountability. Sadly, and inevitably, this has crushed the extent to which staff are in ready-to-receive mode, preventing them from enjoying a valuable feedback process that is both motivating and empowering and enables them to own their next steps and develop their practice.

The real problem is that many of us expect the worst, so during this type of feedback we find it hard to keep an open mind and imagine a scenario where the message we'll receive is a good one. Couple this with the associated language that usually peppers the one-way conversation, and you may be programmed even more into seeking out the negative in the message. Your inner Cynical Caveman tends to associate this feedback format with things going wrong, i.e., impending doom. This approach can push you further back into your cave and further away from the truth. You feel judged based on a limited, external view of your performance. As a result, even if positive comments are shared during the delivery of the salvo, which they often are, you will not hear them with the same clarity. So, how can we change the game?

> ### *A person convinced against her will is of the same opinion still.*
>
> Dale Carnegie – American writer and lecturer

One excellent way of starting is to consider the importance of a shared or common language that is not linked to years of high-stakes accountability and judgement but created by the staff within the school's culture. This will involve working together and exploring alternative ways of phrasing the intention, with the aim to reach a collective agreement on a language that nourishes and acknowledges the school's practice.

Start small and perhaps think about finding alternative words for 'outstanding' or 'observation' and, in doing so, sever the unhelpful cultural links to the past. It certainly seems hard to escape this language. As we mentioned in Chapter Two, the eagle-eyed amongst you will have noticed this very issue within our current Teachers' Standards document, which provides a great example of this type of subtle, negative messaging. It states that teachers need to be "self-critical". What's wrong with "reflective"? We suggest these language changes are not to dumb down expectations but to encourage our talented EduCaveman colleagues to be more receptive to the appraisal process.

> **People want to get recognised for their contributions. They want their work to have meaning. And when you are slacking on recognition, it's essentially the same as ignoring their existence.**
>
> Sabrina Son – content marketing specialist at TINYpulse

Caveman Nuggets

- Outlaw the phrases 'negative feedback' and 'critical feedback' when helping colleagues to develop. These words will just bring down the shutters.
- Develop a school-wide positive language that is agreed upon by the staff and used by everyone engaging in feedback.

We firmly believe that effective feedback should be a shared process. It's a powerful tool and one that the recipients prefer, as it encourages them to participate and to reflect throughout. This is a process in which the recipient is helped to unpick their own practice and identify and own their professional next steps, which, rather than being overwhelming, focuses on a few key points. This type of feedback provides a healthy blend of praise for achievement and agreed suggestions for development.

The relationship is one of parity, in which both parties work together through open dialogue and skilful questioning to identify meaningful and achievable next steps that will help build confidence and more effective teaching or leadership. The age-old alternative of pointing out flaws and providing a set of targets against which the recipient is measured, we would suggest, is less effective, as it can leave the practitioner feeling inadequate and underskilled, reinforcing the negativity bias and edging our caveman back down the continuum.

 Caveman Nuggets

The most important thing to remember with feedback is what they hear, not what you've said.

In our experience, this process is successful when the trust account is high. When there is an abundance of pre-existing trust, the dialogue can be freer. The trust allows room for honesty, and the need to navigate emotions is lessened. Where trust is less evident, and relationships less established, the process can be more charged. So, find ways to oil the cogs through developing those relationships and fostering greater trust.

> ***We all need people who will give us feedback.***
> ***That's how we improve.***
>
> Bill Gates American – business magnate, software developer
> and philanthropist

Of course, there are times when we must give tough, honest or difficult messages. We are no strangers to giving this type of feedback and have done so on many occasions throughout our careers. However, when these times came along and we had to give honest developmental feedback, it was so much easier to deliver because the culture was supportive and strong enough to take it. The feedback in the school was open, regular and a two-way process that everyone trusted. As a result, the feedback was heard and acted upon, and the trust account often remained in surplus.

Our hope is that this chapter should have pulled, or at least eased, the ham from your eyes and provided the incentive to revisit how you, your colleagues and the school might harness the motivational power of feedback for the benefit of everyone in your school community. We also hope that we have given you a fresh perspective on the relationship between monitoring and feedback. Whilst traditional feedback will often only occur after a monitoring event, we encourage you to use feedback at many other times, too. Take time out of your day to deliberately seek out the good stuff and make someone's day by acknowledging and celebrating their hard work and passion. You'll enjoy giving it, they'll enjoy receiving it, and we're confident that in doing so, you'll move along the continuum with a smile on your face.

Giving feedback regularly isn't just beneficial for the employee, it's beneficial for the team, too. Did you know that receiving feedback can actually inspire your employees to work harder and become more engaged? Employees who receive little or no feedback from their managers tend to disengage from their work.

Lindsay Kolowich Cox – blogger and creator of educational content for marketers

Over to You

As we conclude the third part of the triumvirate, we hope that you've enjoyed the opportunity to look at monitoring and feedback through a different lens. In embracing some of the ideas in the first and second parts of Chapter Six, our wish is that the monitoring and feedback process will prove profitable for everyone involved, particularly the children.

Moreover, and perhaps more importantly, we hope that this chapter will prompt you to wear out your shoe leather and seek out the good stuff, with the aim of recognising what a great job the staff around you are doing.

So, there's no time to waste:

- Work as a team to ensure that the giving and receiving of positive informal feedback is a cultural norm in your setting. Practise it, talk about it, do it.
- If you see it, say it. Silence is most definitely not golden.
- If giving praise doesn't come naturally to you, then practise. Start small, perhaps with a thank you, and work your way up from there. The benefits are too great for you to give up.
- You never know: just one piece of unexpected positive feedback from you could trigger a positive chain reaction that may well prevent an outbreak of Malnourished Discretionary Effort (MDE – more of this in the next chapter) and safeguard against the extreme negativity bias. It must start somewhere, so why can't it start with you?

- Get this stuff right and you'll be able to sit back and enjoy the Champion Caveman Culture you have had a hand in creating. You've got nothing to lose and everything to gain, so go for it!

The Intermission

Time-out/Breather
Interlude/La Pausa

Psychologically, intermissions allow [theatre] audiences to pause their suspension of disbelief and return to reality. They are a period during which they can engage critical faculties that they have suspended during the performance itself.

(Wikipedia)

Over every mountain, there is a path, though it may not be seen from the valley.

Theodore Roethke – American poet who, in 1954, won the Pulitzer Prize for Poetry for his book, *The Waking*

 OVER TO BOB...

Well, this hasn't been a performance as such, although while writing this book under various coronavirus 'tier' restrictions and during three national lockdowns, it certainly felt like one at times – for both of us!

We wanted to give you the opportunity to re-engage your critical faculties, take stock and reflect on what you have found useful so far, and how you might adapt or use some of the suggestions and nuggets back at base camp – be that a classroom, staffroom or office. It's another chance to help you out of the valley, to find your 'mountain path' and make further progress on your Caveman journey.

While you're at it, should you be feeling a tad overwhelmed, and perhaps even a little flat, given the content of the last few chapters, we want to use the intermission as an opportunity to remind you about the value of the amazing career path you have chosen. Day in, day out, you give your all to this role with passion and pride, transforming the lives of children and their communities in the process. Sometimes the transformation happens immediately, and sometimes years or even decades later. Whether you are a teacher or a school leader, it is worth stopping for a moment and examining the incalculable depth of your patience, kindness and reservoirs of virtue.

After you have taken that moment (and please do take your time), we want to nudge you, perhaps even push you, towards an important factor on the journey towards achieving and maintaining Champion Caveman Culture. It's an ingredient that we have often hinted at in the book but have yet to make explicit. This factor is implicit in our continuum and is in the hearts and souls of the many people in our profession (you included!); cohorts of dedicated educators who push themselves to achieve the very best for the children in their care. It manifests itself daily as a desire to make a difference, even in the darkest of times. Those who have it are capable of cracking on and going that extra mile whatever the circumstance and whatever is thrown at them, often with a beaming smile. Their moral purpose trumps everything else. Even when sick, they'll drag themselves into work. "The school roof is falling in? Doesn't matter, I'm still teaching maths after playtime."

No one is asking for a medal, and in our experience, no one is consciously attempting to be a martyr; the simple need for betterment guides these incredible individuals. [See figure 4 over the page.]

You see, teaching is unique. It has the power to encourage and bring out the very best attitudes known to mankind. It brings out an irrepressible can-do approach and generates the kind of positivity that gets children bounding into class every day to continue their learning journey with their very own forgotten saint – their Champion Caveman. This makes schools, and ultimately their communities, happier, more rounded places to be. Making a difference, adding value, transforming lives… call it what you will, if you recognise yourself as one of these forgotten saints, now is the time to pause, pour yourself a drink and raise your glass – you deserve it!

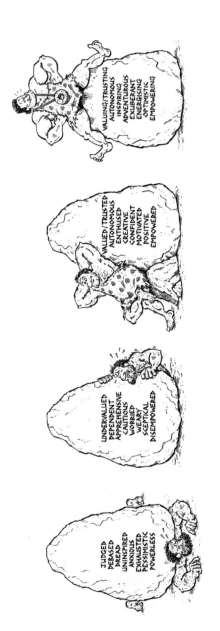

Figure 4: The EduCaveman Continuum – the characteristics of the Cynical, Cautious, Contented and Champion Cavemen

What EduCavemen demonstrate daily across our schools is something often referred to as 'discretionary effort'; a powerful force that goes beyond planning, marking and the general school day. This phenomenon compels staff to complete work well beyond their remit in tackling some of the things we've mentioned in previous chapters, including external validation, initiative overload and continuous change.

When present, discretionary effort ensures that staff not only complete all the many tasks expected of them, and more, but that they offer the extras that go beyond the normal school day: running the school choir; project managing the opening of the school farm from day one to selling farm-fresh eggs; or just simply offering time to mentor challenging children during Tuesday and Friday lunchtime. What's more, this extra work will almost always be done with a smile and with bucket-loads of enthusiasm. Discretionary effort is the glue that binds schools together and elevates an establishment to legendary status among the children and local community. It creates the kind of schools we described in Chapter Four, where the positivity can be detected in the car park, throughout the corridors and beyond.

Discretionary effort within schools is a true tour de force, visible as the enthusiasm, extra effort and application that staff demonstrate daily for the school and the community it serves. Staff apply themselves with boundless energy to everything they do, and often encourage others to join them on their journey. When nurtured, discretionary effort is largely responsible for bustling staffrooms full of individuals who are intrinsically motivated to work harder. It oozes in and around the systems, structures and policies of a school, driving it to be the very best it can be. Wow! So, why do some establishments have this, and how do we encourage it?

Interestingly, for discretionary effort to be alive and kicking in a school, the usual incentives associated with extra endeavour, such as money, rewards or titles can't be applied. At first, this may seem strange, especially when you consider the importance we attach to performance-related pay and the titles now commonplace on any staff who's who list. But we believe discretionary effort has more to do with moral purpose. The stronger this is, the stronger staff engagement becomes. When people can see how their work transforms lives, they will go above and beyond the call of duty without batting an eyelid. Speak to any educator, and you'll find that it's something we intuitively know. It certainly won't be a revelation to anyone working in a school.

But this is where things start to get even more interesting. In some schools we visit, the engagement levels, the willingness of staff to go the extra mile and the abundance of goodwill are simply breathtaking, and for years we've tried to unpick why this is. We think the recipe is relatively straightforward and links directly to our EduCaveman Continuum and each of the chapters in this book. It centres around three factors:

1. The moral purpose
2. The culture
3. The leaders and the team

Put simply, where teachers and leaders are unequivocally clear about why they do what they do (their moral purpose) and are nourished and fed by the school culture and championed or valued within their team (by their colleagues and leaders), the sky really is the limit. We like to call this NDE – nourished discretionary effort – the impact of which can be clearly seen in the characteristics of our Champion Caveman.

Caveman Nuggets

Reflections from previous chapters:

- Wearing out your shoe leather (Chapter Four) is a keystone in encouraging and maintaining discretionary effort.

- Making time to get to know a bit more about your colleagues beyond the classroom is hugely motivational for them. Why not do this regularly and make it part of your culture?

- Being omnipresent as a leader and member of staff is crucial if you want to encourage greater discretionary effort across the school. It's not that difficult; should the opportunity present itself, why not attend the next away netball match, help set out the hall for the Year Seven gym display or drive the minibus to the carol concert at the local care home? I think you get the picture!

- Don't forget to thank colleagues and acknowledge what they are doing for the children and the school. Always look to give regular informal feedback (see Chapter Six, Part III). Remember that silence isn't golden.

- Think about what we said in Chapter Five about how supporting and trusting the staff in our schools is crucial, and the key to nurturing culturally aware schools. This is vital if we are to establish staffrooms full of contented, hopefully even champion staff who are brimming with discretionary effort.

- Where possible, be flexible in your approach and demonstrate goodwill and understanding for those staff who are working well beyond their job description.

Having described the transformational impact of discretionary effort, we want to share a grave concern about the ease with which it can so easily slip under the radar and go unnoticed, uncherished and unloved, especially in schools where silence truly is considered golden and where systems seem to have replaced the need for face-to-face contact. The compelling thing is that, even when the school is blind to the discretionary effort taking place, these superstars will continue to invest time and love into the community they are trying their best to improve and nurture, sometimes single-handedly.

The staff who face these conditions are the SAS of positivity, the 'Duracell Bunnies' of optimism. They work all hours, often to the detriment of their personal lives, to produce and maintain an endless well of hope for others to drink from. In fact, it is clear the only thing keeping these staff members going is the children in front of them and their own motivation to do right by them. Whilst they feel let down by the culture and their colleagues, they limp on, nourished by the connection they feel to the children they teach. But not only that. They suffer acute guilt when they dare to contemplate jumping ship; their innate sense of servitude is compromised as they envisage abandoning their pupils and their community – the very thing that drew them to the profession in the first instance. And so, they squeeze out yet more goodwill – week after week, month after month; perhaps even longer. It may take time, but eventually, like the famous bunnies, our tired cavemen will sadly stop beating their drum.

Staff in these types of establishments may experience what we call MDE – malnourished discretionary effort. Initially, this probably won't affect the status quo, as our elite coterie is made of stern stuff and will carry on regardless. However, if left to wilt, with little or no nourishment, the staff who have played a major part in pushing through the school vision – even initiatives they don't believe in – will eventually run out of steam. This may lead a school into a challenging situation, as the glue we referred to earlier ceases to hold it together. This is so serious that we think it might even have contributed to the recruitment crisis the nation is currently experiencing, as educators leave their profession in droves.

Failure is not fatal, but failure to change might be.

John R. Wooden – American basketball coach

The obvious fact is that if we don't nurture or feed the very people who are propelling our schools to a higher level, we will have problems, no matter how resilient the staff are. These are our heroes, who go one step beyond. We cannot overlook our staff, our most precious resource, especially when motivation is so easy to achieve.

So, why not reflect on the nuggets, strategies and ideas we have discussed so far? These will ensure you stem the tide and avoid an outbreak of MDE, actively encouraging positive, energised staff members to continue in the same vein.

Never confuse a single defeat with a final defeat.

F. Scott Fitzgerald – novelist and screenwriter

Besides considering the power of discretionary effort, one of the most important learning points to embrace from the previous chapters, and particularly the last three, is the theme we return to time and time again, which is the inbuilt nature of some of this stuff. Many of the systems, routines and habits found in schools are so ingrained that even a hot wash with Ariel Bio would struggle to shift them! It's how things have been done for years, and it's often easier not to rock the boat. Building a culture takes time, and breaking it up is just as difficult.

In some schools, the culture is so rigid that the movement towards a new horizon can be daunting and even seem unattainable – a possible result of years of the same leader, the same staff, the same systems or maybe just a lack of vision. In these schools, staff have become trapped in a type of cultural lockdown and respond in a way that feels familiar. Given time, it becomes part of the DNA for all involved, including any newcomers. It seems impossible to contemplate starting a journey, let alone shaking up the status quo. Still, with an emphasis on cultural change, the opportunity for transformation becomes far more likely.

Now, this is where you come in – yes, you! If you have just started at a new school, don't worry – we are not prompting you to overthrow a successful institution in a solo coup. Likewise, if you are a new headteacher or a first-time deputy, we don't want to distract you from wearing out your shoe leather around the school and building relationships. (Just plugging the good stuff...)

Well, the exciting news is that the next bit is up to you. We want you to make a start on the things that have resonated with you so far. Try thanking colleagues around the school more regularly; you could begin by telling them about the things they are doing well and the positive impact they are having. In fact, you could start with any of the many suggestions across the previous chapters – you know it makes sense!

To do this, you will need to train yourself and start turning these new approaches into habits. Now, there is a lot of discussion around retraining yourself to use different approaches and strategies, but what all the research points to is that this kind of change takes time. Some say forty days, others sixty-six, and so on, but I love the argument that the writer and speaker James Clear puts forward in his book *Atomic Habits*; it is so obvious, but such good advice:

> *"At the end of the day, how long it takes to form a particular habit doesn't really matter that much. Whether it takes fifty days or five hundred days, you have to put in the work either way. The only way to get to Day Five Hundred is to start with Day One. So, forget about the number and focus on doing the work."*

The most difficult thing is the decision to act.
The rest is merely tenacity.

Amelia Earhart – aviation pioneer

So, start as soon as you feel comfortable. It will take around ten working weeks for any change to become part of the new way you work. During this time, staff who are awed by your positivity fest may well join your mini revolution.

Even better would be the notion of working together as a team to make a collective change in which creating a different culture in your school becomes the most important focus. When aligned to some of the suggestions in this book, we feel sure it will pay dividends and guarantee an abundance of discretionary effort.

Coming together is a beginning, staying together is
progress, and working together is success.

Henry Ford – founder of Ford Motor Company

So, on with 'The Show'. We hope that you've enjoyed metaphorically munching on your choc ice throughout our short intermission and that it has galvanised your thinking. The five-minute warning bell has rung, and the second act has much to offer – ideas, nuggets, thoughts and discussions that will enhance the importance of developing and planning for more culturally conversant schools.

Chapter 7

Very telling

In this chapter, we'll explore the merits of creating capacity and empowering others through distributed leadership.

The greatest leader is not necessarily the one who does the greatest things. He is the one that gets the people to do the greatest things.

Ronald Reagan – actor and politician who served as 40th President of the United States, 1981-1989

 OVER TO DAVE...

There are many definitions of teaching, but this is the first one I stumbled across on Google: "ideas or principles taught by an authority". There is nothing earth-shattering here, but for the purposes of this chapter, and the next one, this definition helps to bring clarity.

I'd like us to linger on two words from the above definition – 'taught' and 'authority'. For me, the word taught is synonymous with chalk, talk and instruction. Typically, this will involve the dissemination of a particular skill or knowledge from the teacher to the learner. The word authority, I think, simply means a person who is well versed in this skill or knowledge. Nothing new here, then.

However, and here's the interesting bit, I believe that these two words are indelibly printed in the unconscious psyche of all teachers and school leaders, and they would most certainly feature in a national coat of arms created at the Department for Education (or a personal tattoo for the more adventurous). The Google definition has been nurtured and reinforced by the system since as far back as we can remember, from our school days right through to teacher training and onwards to leadership. It's who we are and it's what we do.

While focusing on these two words, it would be remiss of me to overlook a third – 'mentor'. We seem to use this one extensively in education. The role of a mentor can take many guises and, depending on who you talk to, can evoke an array of emotions. Some mentors we remember fondly, some less so... But essentially, mentoring is simply teaching, advising or telling. It's the transference of information from an experienced teacher to a less experienced learner. It's the embodiment of the words taught and authority; a mentor is the ultimate teller.

One might assert that telling is education's modus operandi. We see it daily in our classrooms, with pupils learning new skills that are expertly taught by skilled practitioners. We might see it weekly in staff training sessions, where highly skilled subject specialists impart their expertise in the hope that, in just half an hour, you might pick up how to teach music using the school chime bars to Class 6C. We might also see it during visits from school advisers, in which staff are typically told how they might improve their schools. Education is awash with instruction and unbridled 'telling'. Well, of course it is. After all, we are teachers. So, what exactly is the issue, then?

Most educators are genetically hardwired to teach, tell or mentor, particularly when they are working with colleagues. It is part of our professional conditioning, and it is where we feel most comfortable. It's our 'go-to' mode if you like. If you don't believe me, next time you are at a dinner party and one or more of the guests or the host is a teacher, try lighting the blue touchpaper by asking about the new exams or how good the local school is. We are born to talk without taking a breath until our message is delivered, and without considering whether you might want to contribute. Increasingly, it seems to me that our challenge, both as teachers and as leaders, is to manage this conditioning and make space for additional, equally powerful approaches.

As teachers, I'm sure you'll agree that we do our utmost to marry the blend of direct instruction (or telling) with elicitation – both are equally important. As school leaders, we try hard to ensure that staff development encompasses both mentoring (or 'telling') and coaching (or 'asking'). These are two very different approaches that, when used together, can be transformational.

In the classroom, we are all aware that too much chalk and talk is not conducive to a learner-centred classroom. Moreover, with an exclusive reliance on this approach, independence can wilt away and frustration grow, as we feel we are spoon-feeding our pupils. Sadly, this may result in the joy of learning slipping out of the door unnoticed.

It's barely any different for school leaders, as we aim to balance a directive (or telling) leadership style with more of a coaching approach. With a heavy reliance on the former, we can become disgruntled by our colleagues' apparent lack of initiative or spark, as they tune out the white noise of further instruction.

You don't lead by hitting people over the head – that's assault, not leadership.

Dwight Eisenhower – military officer and statesman who served as 34th President of the United States, 1953-1961

Surely, giving directives or instruction is best saved for military circles, where the environment requires an instant response to an order with little or no thinking, and certainly no dialogue. Yet this approach still makes more than the odd appearance in schools. We then wonder why creativity and risk-taking are in short supply...

My point is that whether we are teachers or leaders, it is important to adopt an approach that encompasses both telling and asking. In the absence of this balanced approach, unbridled telling risks both the staff and pupils feeling neither empowered nor autonomous. I am a classic case in point here – just ask my wife. I have always hated being told what to do. I know, more childhood issues to work through! As quite a creative soul, I love a good dose of free rein. Any sense that I am being 'told' brings out the worst in me. On a particularly bad day, I might even do the opposite of what I am being asked to do.

My wife cottoned onto this very early on in our marriage and now works me like a puppet (string, not glove), giving me the illusion of autonomy, choice and independence. She just asks me a few well-selected questions, I get to exercise a modicum of choice and everyone's a winner. Simple, really.

For several years now, I've strongly believed that our sixth 'Push' factor in the continuum – unbridled telling – is a significant force in schools, and not a particularly helpful one. Along with the five other educational push factors, the systemic telling culture in education can leave our EduCaveman feeling utterly dependent, even powerless.

Just to ensure that my point is not misconstrued, I want to make it clear that of course, there are situations and/or times when both teachers and leaders are required to tell. The most obvious time is when there are concerns about safeguarding. The point I am making relates more to the day-to-day hustle and bustle of school life, and it serves as a reminder to provide others with opportunities to realise their potential and show their worth and value.

In this chapter, and the next one, we will take time to explore how we can manage our built-in urge to 'tell', and move our EduCaveman selves along the continuum towards increased empowerment, autonomy and, ultimately, joy.

Distributed leadership

Over the years, I have been puzzled by the fact that leaders often do more 'telling' as they climb the career ladder. Perhaps this is due to them having to meet the demands of the endless 'mind-in-neutral' tasks referred to in Chapter Three. In my opinion, the reverse should be true, with asking taking preference over telling as you gain more experience and confidence. As I have already mentioned, excessive telling can create staff dependency and leave the leader feeling resentful about their increased workload and their team's lack of initiative.

If this approach is left unchecked in the long term, it can create a dependency culture that is etched into the very fabric of the school. The written-in-stone routines, systems and approaches are hard or even impossible to change, even when they have little or no worth. "We've always done it this way," becomes the mantra. Should one of the school's significant leaders – often the headteacher – leave, chaos will ensue as their replacement tries to work with staff and implement fresh ideas.

Caveman Consideration

Over the course of a normal working day, try to be mindful of the number of times you 'tell' versus the number of questions you 'ask' during your interactions with colleagues.

Were there occasions where, instead of telling, you could have asked a coaching question that might have helped to reduce dependency?

I can certainly recall periods in my career when my creativity, autonomy and independence dwindled (and I am not talking about my time as a financial adviser). When I look back, I can always trace the cause, and often it was the result of being in a team where there was little expectation for me to think for myself. Decisions or instructions were received from above and my job was simply to carry them out. There was no deliberate intention to make me feel disempowered, but nevertheless, this is what happened over time. I questioned why I should bother thinking when the thinking had already been done. If I was tempted to step forward with a new idea or a different approach, a quiet voice in my head would gently remind me that new ideas came from the top down, not the bottom up.

Unwittingly, I began to stop trying. Worse still, my reservoir of natural independence had begun to run dry, and I was developing a sense of reliance or dependency. I awaited my orders like a chick in a nest looking upwards and anticipating its next meal. At the time, it didn't occur to me that I should challenge this scenario. Nor was it strange that when I looked around me, I saw many other chicks looking skyward. This was just how it was. The funny thing is, although my thinking had changed as a team member, my teaching was largely unaffected. I was always mindful of the value of elicitation with my pupils; a good quality question to prompt helpful discussion. I needed to ensure that my pupils took ownership of their learning and were, in the main, the ones doing the work.

One of the greatest things you can do to help others is not just to share and give what you have, but help them discover what they have within themselves to help themselves.

Rita Zahara – celebrity chef, author and entrepreneur

As members of the team stop trying, the burden of responsibility weighing on our leader's shoulders becomes increasingly apparent. There follows the stark, often uncomfortable realisation that there is minimal capacity in the team or system. Even less palatable is the thought that this lack of capacity may have inadvertently been created by too much 'telling'. Eventually, and in the interests of survival, it may seem there is little option but to delegate. After all, how can one person possibly do it all? In my experience, this can often be a time of tension. Staff will have lost confidence, and they will no longer be accustomed to rowing their own boat. (This is a skill that will need practice to master again.) The leader will be desperate for their team to step up but, understandably, they will be rusty. Instead, staff may well be running for the comfort of their own classrooms, probably because it's the one place they feel a sense of autonomy.

I have struggled with the word 'delegation' for as long as I can remember. Instead, I prefer to use the phrase 'distributed leadership'. In my opinion, this is transformational because it involves:

a. the empowerment of others through opportunity and responsibility; if possible, matching skill with organisational need.
b. the joy of watching colleagues grow with their newly embraced responsibility.
c. checking in (not up) every so often, to see how the leader might provide support and offer encouragement.

A central tenet of distributed leadership is to let people get on with what they are good at. If they're good at it, there is little need to tell them what to do. (Remember Bob's story about 50 Squadron earlier in the book?) If and when they get stuck, telling them what to do, for me, would still be a last resort. If they need help, they'll probably speak to somebody who has experience with that role, as Bob did. If support is still needed, a good approach is to ask them questions to help them reach clarity; in other words, adopt more of a coaching approach. (We'll pick this up again in the next chapter when we look at the power of coaching.) This way, autonomy is preserved, empowerment is strengthened and the EduCaveman leader can revel in contributing to the team member's professional growth.

Contrast this with my take on the process of delegation. Whilst my understanding may not be aligned with more mainstream definitions, delegation, for me, is simply the process of a line manager under pressure (and we have all been there) dishing out tasks to their subordinates. Their driving motive is minimising their own workload, with little regard for the development of staff. Line manager support is often absent, or an afterthought at best.

For me, there are huge parallels between the process of distributed leadership and the role of a class teacher. The only small difference is that the leader's pupils take the place of the staff.

The point here is that, through distributed leadership, the EduCaveman leader and teacher can successfully:

- Strengthen empowerment
- Reduce dependency
- Grow trust
- Foster motivation

Just to be clear, the thought that accountability might dwindle under a model of distributed leadership may not hold water. In fact, typically, the reverse can be true. Along with empowerment comes joint and mutual accountability, with staff and pupils enjoying more ownership of their successes, too.

Before we move on, just a little 'health warning' in relation to distributed leadership. Over the years, I have become increasingly aware of a factor that can dilute its positive impact. In light of the extreme negativity bias, this is entirely understandable.

Weary staff are ever mindful of the workload of others. They don't want to weigh down their flagging colleagues with yet more tasks. Whilst this sentiment is totally justified, it can curtail the extent to which staff are empowered through professional opportunity. Because Caveman confidence can be precarious, staff may err on the side of caution and fail to put themselves forward for new responsibilities and opportunities.

Caveman Consideration

Surely part of our role as a coach and/or mentor is to ensure that our colleagues are on the right path?

If you're walking down the right path and you're willing to keep walking, eventually you'll make progress.

Barack Obama – lawyer and academic who served as
44th President of the United States, 2009-2017

When I look back, this was certainly true for me. Although I didn't have the confidence in myself at the time, I am eternally grateful that someone else did. I was blissfully unaware that a good dose of responsibility was exactly what I needed to help me realise my potential and gain greater awareness of my skillset. It also helped me to see that I could rise to the challenge, which in turn gave me greater confidence in my role. When I look back, I can clearly see that this was distributed leadership in action. My head (Bob) had matched a school need with a skill he knew

I had (even if I didn't know I had it at the time). What's more, he intuitively knew that it would boost my confidence and self-belief, and he was right. All I needed was for someone (in this case, Bob) to put me on the right path and encourage me to keep walking...

Caveman Consideration

If the pang of guilt you feel is preventing you from asking a colleague to do something extra, ask yourself these two questions:

- Am I denying them an opportunity to grow professionally?
- Am I denying myself the feeling of gratification as I watch a member of my team grow in confidence and self-belief?

Distributed leadership and perfectionism

In supporting colleagues to empower others and develop their own capacity, I am mindful that the Caveman trait of perfectionism can be a real barrier. As we know from Chapter Two (the extreme negativity bias), many teachers and school leaders have leanings towards perfectionism. If I had a penny for every time I've heard the phrase, "If you want a job done properly, then do it yourself," I'd be a rich man! This mantra, however, is:

a. a barrier to staff empowerment, and
b. the road to resentment – "Why am I the only person working this hard?"

Perfectionism and control often go hand in hand. After all, in the time it takes to explain how to execute a task, you could have done it yourself. This is very tempting when you are time-poor, the stakes are high and you just need to get it done.

At this point, I must admit that I can suffer with the odd bout of perfectionism myself – look no further than my categorised DVD collection and the inside of my car (especially when compared to Bob's!). I won't admonish myself for having high standards, but sometimes the by-products of this trait are culturally unhelpful. But maybe just knowing about your traits and their effect on others is enough.

 ### Caveman Nugget

If you have moments of self-doubt as a Caveman teacher or leader (usually at 3 am), be kind to yourself. If you don't have high standards for your class or your school, then who will?

So, why is the drive for perfection the enemy of team empowerment? I can tackle this best through a worked example.

As a Caveman teacher, you are always chasing your tail, and now you have been asked to put up a display. A member of your team has some release time, and you politely ask them for support. Your colleague obliges, leaving a Post-it note on your desk letting you know it has been done. You can't wait to marvel at the interactive display. You open the classroom door, hoping to be greeted by a vision of beauty, but sadly you are thoroughly underwhelmed. This is the kind of feeling you have on Christmas Day when you open a present to find a pair of socks, but smile gratefully, nonetheless. "How irritating, I should have done this myself," you say to yourself.

Your colleagues think the display was put together by the children – not perfect, but certainly not a disaster.

What I haven't mentioned here is that your colleague is greatly lacking in confidence. The fact that they have even agreed to help is excellent progress for them. They fear not getting it right and, therefore, are risk averse. They rarely put their head above the parapet. You know what's coming, don't you?

You pop in to see your colleague at the end of the day and, with irritation as your driver, make some fairly cutting jibes about the smorgasbord of crepe paper attached half-heartedly to your wall. Obviously, this team member now feels even less confident. Their propensity to take risks was already low and now it has all but vanished. In terms of empowerment, autonomy and feeling valued, I think it's fair to say the situation has substantially regressed.

So, what's the alternative? A good starting point is something I picked up from a friend: lower your expectations and raise your game. Admittedly, my instant gut reaction to this phrase was one of intense dislike. After all, I don't want to lower my standards. Why should I?

 Caveman Nugget

Lower your expectations and raise your game.

So, let's add a couple of phrases to see how we perfectionists can get this phrase working for us: lower your *(short-term)* expectations and raise your *(team's long-term)* game. My long-term aim here is to ensure every one of my team members feels trusted and valued. My strong wish is for them to feel empowered and comfortable with taking risks – in short, Champion Caveman

Culture. I want them brimming with confidence and feeling connected to our team vision. If this can happen, the need for me to be involved in short-term low-stakes issues should lessen greatly, as they will have the confidence and the competence to work through challenges independently. They will know they are trusted to get on with things.

So, with the display example in mind, perhaps I need to focus less on the short game (a perfect display) and more on building up my team.

Glory lies in the attempt to reach one's goal and not in reaching it.

Mahatma Gandhi – Indian lawyer who led his country to freedom from British colonial rule

Okay, so the display was not completed to my (possibly obsessive-compulsive) high standards, but it is one less thing on my to-do list and my colleague has grown in confidence as they feel trusted and appreciated. In fact, it transpires that they enjoy putting up displays and have noticed that the one in the school hall is looking a little dated. They ask if they can indulge their newfound talent, and off they go. Unsurprisingly, it doesn't meet with my impossible standards, but, by the average Joe's benchmark, they've done a sterling job, and more trust and confidence has been built in the process.

And so, you can see that a slight refocus (from short game to long game) may well yield improved organisational capacity and a stronger culture. Forgive the crude example, but I think it helps to capture the essence of our message.

Practise hands-off management as much as possible and hands-on management as much as necessary.

Ken Blanchard – American author, business consultant and motivational speaker

A word of caution here. The display example involved a low-stakes task. With higher-stakes tasks, perhaps there would be merit in sitting down first with the team member and having a discussion to reach a shared agreement about the desired outcome. This will manage everyone's expectations.

If the result does not pass muster, perhaps a frank conversation to address the short game is needed. However, with increased trust in the account, one would hope for minimal damage to confidence and trust.

So, lower your (*short-term*) expectations and raise your (*team's long-term*) game. Through focusing on your team's long-term success, you may, in the end, tackle the short-term challenges whilst also watering down the culture of dependency.

We have now covered the benefits of distributed leadership and the dangers of perfectionism. What else can we do to minimise the possible negative impact of unbridled 'telling'?

You can start to build a 'coaching' culture that inspires and empowers others. We'll take a closer look at the transformational longer-term impact of coaching in the next chapter, Just Ask ...

Over to You

Take a look at your to-do list or the tasks you regularly undertake during a normal working day. Are there aspects of your role that you are doing out of habit?

Can you set aside some time to consider who might be better placed to carry out some of these tasks? Whilst you might not be ready or comfortable with letting go of the reins, can you loosen your grip?

As a teacher, are you doing things that your pupils could quite easily do themselves? Which pupils would embrace some extra responsibility and grow as a result? Empower them and enjoy watching them relish the opportunity.

As a leader, are there members of your team who would flourish given a little more opportunity? For instance, are there quieter team members who are just as ambitious but may find it harder to step up? Can you find a way to identify and empower them?

In relation to low-stakes tasks, and on a scale of zero to ten, how comfortable are you with lowering your standards in the shorter term to build confidence and enhance capacity in the longer term? What actions might you take to become more comfortable with a change in your short game?

Chapter 8

Just Ask...

In this chapter, we'll explore the power of coaching to unlock the potential within.

 ## OVER TO DAVE...

Chacun voit midi à sa porte

Literal translation: *Everyone sees noon at his door.*

This exquisite French phrase means we are all engrossed in our own views, beliefs and opinions. What's more, we consider them to be true.

In a nutshell, we've all got our own take on the world, and we believe we are right.

If you were to ask any teacher or school leader to explain what they want for their staff or pupils, they'd look you in the eye and say something straight from the heart, such as, "We want them to feel empowered, valued, trusted and autonomous."

If you were then to ask them what they want for themselves, the chances are the answer would be equally heartfelt, and possibly even identical.

The interesting bit comes with a third question: how do you actually feel in your role? I suspect the answer would be more aligned with the characteristics at the left-hand extreme of our continuum – a far cry from the aspiration of Contented, or even Champion, Caveman status.

At the very heart of the previous chapter was the determination to help bridge this gap. However, that was only part of the story in relation to how we can build capacity in teams, schools and our systems through the empowerment of our colleagues. In this chapter, we'll look at how a coaching approach can supplement and further cement the ideas and nuggets previously explored. After all, it's a tool with the huge potential to bring about or strengthen cultural transformation and lessen the impact of the extreme negativity bias.

Coaching is one of the most misused words in education. I hear it used continually, but so often it doesn't accurately describe the user's approach. Let me clarify this with a discussion between two colleagues.

"Did you have a good afternoon?"

"I did. I was coaching my trainee."

"Excellent. What were you discussing?"

"I was advising her on effective behaviour management strategies."

"Okay. How?"

"Well, I was chatting through my list of top ten approaches, which I've developed over the years."

"Did she find it useful?"

"Absolutely. She didn't say a word. She just seemed in awe of me and my list..."

This exchange seems more akin to mentoring or 'telling' than it does coaching. With the very best intentions, the more seasoned member of staff in the scenario was imparting her accumulated wisdom to her trainee and acting as the 'expert'. Did she take into account that the trainee might already have some of the answers, strategies and solutions within her already? Possibly not. Okay, let's really get under the skin of coaching.

Coaching is the art of facilitating the performance, learning and the development of another.

Myles Downey – one of the world's leading practitioners and thinkers in business coaching

Myles very neatly captures the essence of coaching here. In fact, it was this very quote that propelled me to find out more about it and to begin my own coaching journey. In 2006, I picked up a book that permanently changed my thinking. It was called *Coaching for Performance* by Sir John Whitmore. Not only did the guidance in this book permeate my professional approach, but it also positively impacted my personal life, too – particularly my relationships.

> **We have two ears and one mouth so that we can listen twice as much as we speak.**
>
> Epictetus – Greek philosopher

If you were to speak with my wife or my close friends, I am confident the consensus would be that I am now a much better listener. What's more, through using coaching questions, I am better able to help my friends untangle their thinking, which often enables them to feel more empowered, confident and energised.

The best and most succinct way I can explain the difference between coaching and mentoring is this: coaching is asking, mentoring is telling. If you adopt a coaching approach, you seek to empower the person you are working with. You assume that the solution to the challenges they face resides inside them.

> **Coaching is unlocking a person's potential to maximise their own performance. It is helping them to learn, rather than teaching them.**
>
> Sir John Whitmore – pioneer of the executive coaching industry

You may recall Bob touching on this in Chapter Six, Part I. He explained that a coach is not acting as an expert but comes to the conversation offering a service. A coach acts as an equal partner, a sounding board and a mirror for the colleague to share their perception of reality and articulate their own solutions and ways forward. The role of a coach is more akin to that of a facilitator. Through powerful and deliberate questioning, a coach can elicit the solution(s) from their coachee or unlock their potential.

Caveman Consideration

A coaching culture can have a transformational impact on individuals, teams, organisations and, ultimately, the education system. Through a coaching approach, staff and organisations can experience greater empowerment and confidence. This can often be coupled with increased energy and strengthened commitment to action.

When working one to one, coaching is an effective tool in supporting a coachee to develop greater clarity of thinking in relation to:

- Goals
- Solutions and/or actions to meet current challenges
- Knowledge of self – in particular, one's strengths
- Understanding of others – their words, actions and motives

(We cover these last two points in more detail in Chapter Nine.)

So, in practical terms, what might a coaching session involve?

- Time to develop trust and rapport between the coach and the coachee.
- Active listening to strengthen the coach/ coachee relationship and build trust.

- Deliberate and planned questioning to prompt deeper reflection.
- The identification of goals.
- Coach perceptivity or discernment – this may well come naturally, but it will often take time and practice to improve.
- Giving developmental and positive feedback.

The repertoire of skills required to be an effective coach is, therefore, quite sophisticated. It may well take some time to become proficient, and it can often require a commitment to training from the outset.

What are the rules of the 'coaching game'?

- No judgement; sessions can provide a safe space to let off steam and express concerns/ worries.
- Confidentiality to preserve trust.
- Time for reflection; there may well be awkward silences – this is when the learning happens!
- The guiding agenda is the coachee's success.
- Coaching is a non-directive process, with the coachee owning their next steps.

There are many definitions of the coaching process, but I feel these points will give you a strong flavour of what it is and, perhaps more importantly, the benefits it may bring.

Health warning

Be careful not to confuse coaching with instructional coaching. Unlike coaching, instructional coaching (mentoring) will, typically, involve the coach acting as an expert, identifying possible targets from the outset and the strategies/small steps the coachee (in this case, the teacher or staff member) will need to take to reach them. The instructional coach often takes full responsibility for helping the teacher to practise and learn these new strategies through modelling, observation of others and direct feedback. The connection between the instructional coach and teacher is regular, builds trust and supports the individual's development (see Chapter Six, Part I for further clarification).

Before a coaching session, I will typically remind myself that the guiding agenda for the session is my coachee's success. This helps me to fight my natural instinct to 'help' with advice, or telling. I try hard, where I can, to leave judgment at the door and to be mindful that – as the quote at the start of this chapter pointed out – "everyone sees noon at their door".

> **_Seek first to understand and then be understood._**
>
> Dr Stephen Covey – American educator, author, businessman and keynote speaker

On the occasions when I forget myself, an in-built mechanism pushes Dr Covey's wise words to the forefront of my mind.

When I'm working with people, from trainee teachers to CEOs, I mainly assume that they hold within themselves the solutions to any challenges they are experiencing and discussing with me. It's my job to elicit these through careful questioning and active listening. Why can't the person you are working with be the authority, especially given that it is their school, their culture, their 'true north'? After all, it is their problem or challenge, and I am merely a guest in their workplace. The moment I sort it out or solve it, I am fostering a relationship of dependency.

Occasionally, when I am working with schools that are in a tight spot with little time, I revert to a more instructional/mentoring approach. I take on the role of the expert, but where possible, I provide a menu of options to ensure there is a degree of ownership and autonomy. If I am asked which option I would choose, I will, of course, express my preference. However, this is not my preferred way of working.

My point is that I try, where I can, to live by my professional mantra and ask more and tell less. It's as simple as that.

If you're like most people, you probably seek first to be understood; you want to get your point across. And in doing so, you may ignore the other person completely, pretend that you're listening, selectively hear only certain parts of the conversation or attentively focus on only the words being said but miss the meaning entirely. So why does this happen? Because most people listen with the intent to reply, not to understand. You listen to yourself as you prepare in your mind what you are going to say, the questions you are going to ask, etc. You filter everything you hear through your life experiences, your frame of reference. You check what you hear against your autobiography and see how it measures up. And consequently, you decide prematurely what the other person means before he/she finishes communicating.

Dr Stephen Covey

Ask more and tell less...? So, what exactly do I mean?

My aim is to facilitate the thinking and learning of the people I work with. I consider telling to be the poor relation of asking. A person's commitment to action is far stronger if they own their solutions or next steps.

The success of the retired international hockey player Alex Danson, a double Olympic medallist who helped her team to win gold when they represented Great Britain in Rio in 2016, is an excellent illustration of this crucial last point.

When she was younger and trying to break into the England hockey team, the manager challenged her to improve her fitness and stamina in matches. So, she asked her father to wake her up every morning to go out for a run. He refused; however, he did promise that if she were to knock on his door, he would join her no matter what the weather. This subtle difference encouraged a far greater commitment to action from Alex. The rest, as they say, is history.

For me, empowering colleagues through a coaching approach is generally preferable and, in my experience, can result in powerful and longer-term changes that can build both confidence and capacity in teams and organisations.

A good coach is positive. Your job when coaching is not correcting mistakes, finding fault and assessing blame. Instead, your function is achieving goals by coaching your staff to peak performance. Focusing on the positive means that you start with what's good and what works, and spend your attention and energy there.

Marshall Cook – business author, and Laura Poole
– associate certified coach

You can see, therefore, that coaching involves a vastly different approach to mentoring. No better, no worse – just different. Whilst some teachers may naturally use a coaching approach, typically, it can go against the grain. It did for me as a teacher, and for a while it felt excruciatingly uncomfortable. I can remember my early cynicism – "I'm a teacher, for goodness' sake; I am here to teach. You can't just keep asking questions!"

Despite myself, I persisted, and when working with pupils and staff, I deliberately took a stance of curiosity. I made a concerted effort to *ask more and tell less.*

My absolute conversion and commitment to the coaching approach was sealed when I began to see my staff growing in confidence and autonomy, which gave me great joy. Shortly after that, I made another mental link, which was a genuine personal eureka moment.

A colleague (I can't remember who) once said to me: *"We want our classrooms to be full of independent, self-regulating learners. Our job is, essentially, to make ourselves redundant."*

I must admit, I found this idea somewhat strange at first. The notion of redundancy was not particularly palatable, and it definitely had an impact on my teacher ego. However, I eventually acquiesced and later fully embraced this idea. It is still a central tenet of my thinking and one I hold dear. Anyway, my point is this: as a leader who was rather wet behind the ears, the penny finally dropped when I realised that my colleague's quote rang true for adults, too. Just substitute 'classrooms' for 'staffrooms': *"We want our staffrooms to be full of independent, self-regulating learners. Our job is, essentially, to make ourselves redundant."*

I am an impassioned advocate of coaching and truly believe in its power to transform organisational culture, nowhere more so than in education. Having embraced and used coaching as a tool since the early noughties, I can't think of a more potent medicine to lessen the cultural damage inflicted by the two issues we explored in Chapter Two – the extreme negativity bias and the deficit model of education. For exhausted staff, a coaching culture that focuses on solutions, positivity and finding strength may well be an attractive option, and it is certainly in keeping with the message that flows through our book. We want to break dependency and foster autonomy and empowerment.

But does all this seem a little idealistic? Well, perhaps...

Coaching and the reality of school life

I would like to spend a little time here examining how the introduction of a coaching approach may rub up against the reality of school life. In my view, this is something that doesn't get sufficient coverage. If we can acknowledge the possible challenges of introducing a coaching culture to school life, we can plan to better meet those challenges.

Coaching demands time. Teachers, leaders and schools don't have it. More than anything, staff crave just one thing – more time. Time in schools is a real scarcity. I often joke with colleagues and ponder what the phenomenon of clock-watching must be like. For just one day, wouldn't it be nice to be bored! Coaching seems to work most effectively when the coachee has the time and the head space to really reflect and think more deeply. Some of our best creative thinking comes to the fore during school holidays, when we are no longer consumed by the frenetic pace of school life. This could happen in the shower or when we are having a beer with friends – see Chapter 10. It takes a disciplined, school-based coach and coachee to ring-fence this time and allow for such thinking. Many of my colleagues have made this work, but they all agree that it takes discipline. If time is short, and the coach thinks they have the solution or answer to a colleague's challenge or problem, the temptation to provide advice can be too great to resist. Indulging in the temptation will, in the eyes of the coach, not only save precious time but will also make them feel good, which is great if they are afflicted with the extreme negativity bias. But as soon as this happens, as well meaning as it is, we have made a retrograde step in relation to dependency. So, lack of time in schools can be a real obstacle to effective coaching.

Coaching is non-directive. We covered this point comprehensively in the previous chapter, but I can't overstate its importance – nothing like a bit of over-learning! Typically, teachers and school leaders can be genetically hardwired to work from an instructional basis, so telling and/or advising can be our default setting. After all, this is what the system has modelled to us from inception. Broadly speaking, I would assert that the art of coaching is facilitation. Some of the most effective teachers I work with are masters of facilitating their pupils' learning. So, they may not say a huge amount, but they use planned and deliberate questioning to stimulate deeper understanding. However, when working with fellow colleagues, these adept facilitation skills seem to get packed away in favour of a more 'telling' approach, often unconsciously. I'm not sure why this is, but perhaps when working with other adults, staff return to their instructional comfort zone. This is a casual observation and perhaps I'm wrong, but I do come across it time and again in the course of my work. To me, it's a baffling phenomenon, as the question is more powerful than the answer.

The tension between school appraisal and staff development through coaching. Many school-based coaches are school leaders who also assume line management responsibilities. School appraisal systems can often be high-stakes, top-down and focused on deficits and gaps. The onus can be on the staff to prove their performance, and this can undermine and erode trust (see Chapter Six, Part II).

Conversely, coaching is a very different process. There is a balance of power, and the guiding agenda is the coachee's success. Effective staff development through coaching requires trust and rapport between both parties. Will this trust be eroded if the same leader is also carrying out the role of line manager using the appraisal model I have just described? There is good reason to think that it might. Often, during coaching sessions, the temptation to the coach to obliquely address school improvement priorities is too great, and in that moment the session agenda moves away from the coachee and back to the 'manager' or the organisation. I'm sure it can work, but the tension between line management and development through coaching requires careful navigation. My experience is that the blurring of the two processes can undermine both.

Caveman Consideration

I'd like to know if there is any quantitative or qualitative data that attests to the effectiveness or otherwise of the traditional model of school appraisal to effect meaningful and positive change in Caveman performance? I wonder if a coaching or developmental model might yield improved outcomes? Just a thought...

Schools may be nursing a cultural hangover. In all schools, leaders will come and go. Each leader will bring with them their own unique style and way of working. I sometimes work with school leaders who are experiencing what I have coined a 'cultural hangover'. This is a very real scenario in which their leadership style and way of working is so diametrically different from their predecessor that it is the cause of short-term confusion for the staff. The current leader may use a largely coaching style, preferring to ask more and tell less. However, for a decade prior to this, the staff may have been accustomed to a more commanding style, which focused largely on directives as opposed to direction. Initially, staff may be sceptical of the fresh opportunities afforded to them, as well as the new approach being used. They may be unaccustomed to the levels of trust on offer and wonder whether their colleagues are embracing this new way of working. You see, after years of being force-fed initiatives that come 'flat packed' with their own instructions, it might be hard to learn to trust again. The new leader may be genuinely baffled by the extent of staff dependency, but, nonetheless, will continue to serve 'cultural fry-ups' to help nurse the hangover.

Anyway, it is 12.15 on a Monday afternoon. The new leader finishes their work for the morning and decides to head to the canteen for lunch. They open their office door to be greeted by a huge queue of staff who, unfamiliar with the new culture, seek instruction and reassurance for an array of low-stakes decisions. For a moment, the leader forgets herself and wonders who these staff queuing to see her are. The dependency is palpable. Eventually, after several years of fostering a coaching culture, the dependency weakens and gives way to an alternative way of doing things, in which the staff embrace responsibility, welcome risk and are largely autonomous. The Caveman coaching culture is both alive and rich. Over time, mentoring becomes a dirty word. The near-tyranny of the previous regime was so oppressive that the diametrically opposite model will always be a hit. But here's my point: effective schools and staff know when and how to utilise both. Coaching has its place, and so does mentoring. However, given the extreme negativity bias, it is easy to see why coaching is an attractive approach. My advice (yes, advice!) is to be discerning over when the use of coaching will be most powerful in your school journey – then it will serve you well.

Caveman Nugget

Effective organisations utilise coaching and mentoring. They know when and how to use both.

Well-meaning missed opportunities. When working with schools and discussing the subject of coaching, I am often told by staff that their respective headteachers will say, "Don't bring me problems, bring me solutions." Whilst the commitment to an empowered and independent staff is evident in this phrase, it may prevent the opportunity for a useful coaching conversation.

In his book, *The Coaching Habit*, Michael Bungay Stanier, an author and keynote speaker, describes what he calls the AWE question – *'And What Else?'* He advocates asking this question at least three times to tease out wisdom, insight and more possibilities. By only asking staff to bring solutions, the coach may miss out on a useful coaching conversation.

Caveman Consideration

So, in practical terms, what is the format or structure for a one-to-one coaching session? Well, these sessions can take many different forms; however, I like to use the popular and easy-to-follow GROW model, created by Sir John Whitmore. GROW is an acronym, and it stands for:

> **Goal** – goals and aspirations.
>
> You might ask: "What is your goal related to this issue?"

Realities – current situation, internal and external obstacles.

You might ask: "What is moving you towards your goal?"

Options – possibilities, strengths and resources.

You might ask: "What different kind of options do you have to achieve your goal?"

Wrap-up – actions and accountability.

You might ask: "On a scale of one to ten, how committed are you to taking each of these actions?"

By going through these four key stages (which may or may not be in this order), the coachee can achieve a clearly defined result.

As I've said before, coaching has transformed my thinking and my approach. If you want continued professional development for your staff, I can think of no better investment. It is both personalised and powerful, and for me, it is a must for a school's cultural development plan. If executed well, Champion Caveman Culture beckons... Go on, go for it!

Over to You

If what you've read has whet your appetite, it may be time to start thinking about how you might introduce a coaching culture (or further strengthen the culture that already exists).

This could be within your team, department, school or even system; whatever you feel is appropriate. The introduction of such a different way of working might call for a staged approach, and there is no perfect process. However, I hope the following suggested stages might prove useful in kicking things off.

Stage 1

When the team is transitioning from one approach to another, there will inevitably be times when unbridled 'telling' rears its head again, particularly if the team is under pressure.

From the outset, ensure that a shared agreement is reached about the need to challenge a person's approach if it doesn't fit with the team's shared vision. In other words, if someone's approach is overly autocratic, the expectation is that this will be addressed and replaced with a coaching approach. Given the shared commitment to a coaching model, this hopefully won't incite too many difficult conversations.

Stage 2

Through consultation with staff, reach a shared agreement about which coaching model you will adopt. I have mentioned the GROW model, but there are other equally powerful ones out there. Train the staff on how to use the model and ensure a shared vernacular.

Stage 3

Catch your staff being good, or, as we like to say, 'be more dog'. In much the same way that we adopt this approach to manage the behaviour of pupils in our classrooms, the same applies in recognising good practice in relation to staff and the new model. Make time in staff or departmental meetings to recognise and celebrate good practice, such as instances when staff have chosen to ask more and tell less. This will reinforce effective coaching and colleagues will experience growing independence and appreciate the power of a well-planned question to foster greater autonomy.

Stage 4

Ring-fence time. Create coaching partners and provide time for coaching sessions to take place. Encourage discussion about the positive outcomes as a result of coaching; there is no need for details, but there is merit in sharing when and where it has proved a valuable process. Celebrate instances where impromptu informal coaching interactions have been helpful in moving people's thinking forward.

Stage 5

Make time to discuss 'health warnings' around coaching; we've already touched on some of them. Sometimes, the pairing of coaching partners may not work out and you'll need to adjust accordingly. Moreover, if a line of questioning is simply not working, it is OK for the coachee to request a menu of possible options (providing, of course, the coach has made it clear they have stepped out of coaching mode and are now in mentor mode).

As with the adoption of all new approaches, there will be teething issues; these are to be expected and, to some degree, welcomed, as they allow for adjustments and tweaks. Keep reviewing the process so that it is fit for purpose.

There is no perfect model and the process can be murky at times. This is par for the course. Stick with it, have fun, and I have every confidence that you will observe dwindling dependency and a happier, more empowered team.

Chapter 9
The Inner Work

In this chapter, we'll explore 'The Big Four' – trust, self-awareness, vulnerability and courage.

Erst denken, dann handeln

Translation: *First think, then act.*

This succinct and poignant German proverb is a helpful reminder, when things are hotting up, to pause and think. It encourages us to *respond* and not to *react*. A chosen or considered response can often yield a more fruitful outcome.

 ## OVER TO DAVE...

I was chatting to a colleague recently and, out of the blue, she asked me a very simple yet powerful question: "When are you at your best?"

I can't remember my exact response, and I don't think I was particularly articulate, but it is a question I have been exploring in my mind ever since, and one that has prompted a huge amount of reflection on my working life to date. I guess by 'best' she meant when do I feel most valued, adventurous and inspired? When am I energised, empowered and feeling like a true Champion Caveman?

In pondering her question, one thing is clear to me. I love people and I love being part of a team. It's what gives me my energy. As I think back over my career, the good times, when I was at my best, were without exception when I was working as part of a highly effective team. I was free to drop my shoulders, relax, think freely, be creative and enjoy the moment. This gave me more than enough reason to get out of bed in the morning.

So, what exactly do I mean by a highly effective team? The phrase is quite vague, so let's explore it in a little more detail.

The teams that I recall most fondly had members who were entirely comfortable with their professional 'gaps' or areas of weakness. These were the sort of colleagues who could talk openly and honestly to each other, and anyone else for that matter, about their workplace foibles. They wouldn't bat an eyelid at discussing how they found certain issues difficult and had no fear of judgment or ridicule – they simply oozed humility. Furthermore, they could say sorry at the drop of a hat and genuinely mean it. My point here is that they were entirely comfortable with showing professional vulnerability and learning from others. For me, working in a team like this was wholly liberating. Empowering even. I found that any professional pretence ebbed away and that I quickly felt comfortable in my own skin and could get on with, and excel at, my role.

It didn't take me long to notice or learn that these types of team members want nothing different for their teammates. In role modelling professional vulnerability, they give unspoken permission to the other members of the team to be more comfortable with their deficiencies. Knowingly or unknowingly, they foster a culture of minimal judgement, authenticity and trust. Over a short period, other members of the team cease trying to conceal their vulnerabilities, safe in the knowledge that the people around them will also have professional weaknesses. They begin to feel more secure in their roles and start to focus on their strengths and how these might be useful to the team. Whilst doing this, they also feel comfortable enough to learn from their colleagues. Teams like this seem effortless in their workings.

Caveman Nugget

Show a little professional vulnerability from time to time.

With this change in focus, team members know exactly what strengths they bring to the table, and they deliberately play to them. They also encourage, and sometimes demand, that other team members do the same. As the team grows in effectiveness, members enjoy giving credit to their colleagues and celebrating their joint progress.

I contend that this pivotally important trait is a hard one to find in EduCavemen, and I find this extremely sad. We spend so much time shining a light on the aspects of our practice that fall short, and working to improve them, that we can forget about the other skills within our toolkit that are polished and begging to be utilised. These are the ones we should feel proud to possess. In fact, in my experience, due to the extreme negativity bias, and because we rarely, if ever, discuss these attributes, we can even cease to see and believe that we are highly proficient in many areas of our working lives. And worst of all is that when we do dare to share with others those areas where we might excel, there is paralysing discomfort and/or awkwardness, as our inner Caveman voice murmurs that we need to curb our boastfulness.

There's a huge difference between arrogance and being at one with our strengths. As a profession, I strongly believe we need to be much clearer about this if we are to progress along the continuum towards our goal of Contented and even Champion Caveman Culture. Ask a teacher or school leader what they need to work on, and you'll be there for hours as they look inward, reflect and forensically break down their weaknesses. In fact, you may well need to pull up a camp bed at this point and have a touch typist note down the many points that will be flying at you without a breath being drawn. Conversely, ask a teacher or school leader where they excel and watch the conversation dry up in seconds. Even if you were to employ an expert team of interrogators from the special services to assist, little would be forthcoming. If this wasn't true, it would be funny – but sadly, it is a very real and stark cultural indicator.

 Caveman Nugget

Set aside regular time with a trusted colleague and take it in turns to share your professional strengths. For these sessions, ban any talk of weakness!

Anyway, to move on... We were talking about the teams and colleagues who deliberately play to their professional strengths and who encourage other team members to do the same, which is very much how Bob's 50 Squadron team behaved (see Chapter Five). Let's take a moment to look at what happens in teams where this takes place as a matter of course. We have a high-performing team who:

1. Know each other inside out
2. Unreservedly accept each other
3. Play to their strengths
4. Enjoy working together
5. Manage conflict
6. Are comfortable working intuitively
7. Make sound judgements

If you have ever worked in a team like this, you'll know how fulfilling it is. You will have experienced team members who embrace the notion that, given the trust that exists, it is better to ask for forgiveness than to ask for permission. Within this team, you'll have seen a strong culture form, which embraced honesty and authenticity and could withstand, and even demand, regular ongoing feedback. It's a nice place to be – joyous, even. It's a place to grow professionally and to be your very best; a place where trust is in abundance.

Caveman Consideration

Think of a team you belong to. Now score it from zero (absent) to ten (fully present) on each of the seven characteristics listed on the previous page.

What are your next steps as a team?

Shall we explore the alternative? It pains me to do so, as I'm sure it pains anyone who has ever been part of the 'closed shop' I am about to describe, but it will help to emphasise my point.

Think of a team whose members are less inclined to share their gaps. A team in which none of the members:

- Admits to finding anything difficult.
- Seems to have any deficiencies.
- Is comfortable with showing professional vulnerability.

This kind of team can seem, or can portray themselves as, bulletproof; superhuman, even.

They sound like a wonderful bunch, don't they? Well, I would suggest that working in a team like this may be an entirely different experience to the previous scenario. You may not feel like you can show any vulnerability and you may stop taking risks through fear of what might happen if you make a mistake. You may even start to conceal your gaps and begin to feel insecure, avoiding the urge to volunteer information or get involved at any cost, as you actively seek out the shadows and the cubby holes of the staffroom during meetings. You may no longer feel trusted, and your trust in colleagues may begin to dissipate, as you secretly wonder who might be judging you...

So, what's my point?

Whatever your position or role within a school, being authentic and true to yourself is key. By role modelling a little vulnerability, you give others – adults and pupils alike – permission to be themselves too, which inevitably helps to foster greater trust. It will take a degree of Caveman courage, but the benefits will surely be worth it. They really will.

With each chapter, we have been piecing together our cultural jigsaw, and this final piece – trust – might well take centre stage in our puzzle. It links with many of the other pieces and may be pivotal when managing the extreme negativity bias and helping our Cynical or Cautious Caveman along the continuum.

As we know, the Champion Caveman feels trusted and, what's more, he trusts his team. And it is perhaps this feeling, more than any other, that enables him to be the very best he can be. He thoroughly enjoys his role and is a highly effective member of his team.

You will recall that we touched on the pivotal importance of trust in Chapter Three, when I described the culture that existed within my favourite class. I went on to explain that, as a team, my pupils and I worked really hard to foster and develop that trust over the course of the year; it was the result of many positive emotional interchanges.

*When the trust account is high, communication is easy,
instant and effective.*

Dr Stephen Covey

Sadly, over recent decades, the educational 'push' factors within
the continuum, which we outlined in Chapter Two, have tested
the limits of trust within our profession, and in many cases may
have broken it unequivocally. Consequently, it becomes easy to
see how once you are at this end of the continuum, you may feel
judged or debased. It is likely that you won't feel trusted, nor will
you trust your team, or the system for that matter.

Your workplace may not be a place where you can be
professionally vulnerable. You may find yourself in self-
protective mode and keeping your head below the parapet – you
have to be. In this high-stakes, immediate-impact culture, any
hint of weakness will be sniffed out and tackled.

The Cynical Caveman workplace is not a place where
shortcomings are freely volunteered. Imagine, if you will, a
typical weekly staff meeting. Some training is delivered at
the end of a busy teaching day, and more than a few staff are
struggling to process the intricacies of this new pedagogy. This
is probably because, amongst other things, they are not in ready-
to-receive mode (see Chapter Three). Anyway, at the end of
the meeting, the trainer asks the team, as usual, if everything
has been understood. The Cynical Caveman scans the room
desperately looking for colleagues who are also perplexed, but
sadly, he cannot meet anyone's eye and affirm that he is not
alone. At this point, he assumes that he is the only member of the
team who hasn't understood any of the content delivered within
the last hour. (I think we have all been there!)

Will they raise their hand and volunteer their complete lack of understanding to everyone else in the team? Not on your Caveman nelly! The stakes are too high. Better to say nothing than to risk showing any vulnerability. After all, who would want to do that in the full gaze of others?

So, how can we start building this much needed trust so that all staff can feel comfortable enough to be honest, professionally vulnerable and have the courage to ask for support or development?

The Trust Triangle

Trust has three drivers: authenticity, logic and empathy. When trust is lost, it can almost always be traced back to a breakdown in one of them. To build trust as a leader, you first need to figure out which driver you 'wobble' on.

Frances Frei – Harvard Business School professor leadership coach and executive founder of the Leadership Consortium

Before we address this question, it might be helpful to explore the Trust Triangle in the quote above, as it emphasises the message in our chapter, and indeed our book, by highlighting the importance of maintaining authenticity, logic and empathy when developing and maintaining successful teams.

So, what exactly do we mean by authenticity, logic and empathy?

- Authenticity means that people genuinely feel that they know the real you.
- Logic means people believe that you are on the right path and taking the right steps.
- Empathy means that people believe you're in it for everyone.

Should one of these drivers 'wobble', it would be easy to see how any carefully built trust might start to erode. In the context of this chapter, we can begin to see the importance of authenticity, which may be strengthened through self-awareness.

Caveman Consideration

What's your 'wobble'?

How will you stabilise it?

Looking back at my various roles, the 'wobble' that springs to mind most vividly is empathy, and I can see why. Teachers and leaders are always squeezed for time. They may have minimal capacity to think about, let alone demonstrate, empathy, and this could be why some staff choose to deal with the 'business' of the school while avoiding the slightly messier unpredictability of relationships.

It is easy to say, but if you can find more time to connect and listen to your colleagues (or wear out your shoe leather), there is a stronger likelihood you will be able to tackle this wobble.

The logic 'wobble' tends to bubble to the surface when people have misgivings or are unclear about the team's vision. Given that a shared vision is a fundamental element for successful change (see Chapter Five), this can be very challenging to deal with. Couple this with ineffective team communication and the logic wobble may well be amplified.

However, in our experience, the most challenging wobble to settle is often authenticity. In the context of the extreme negativity bias, and the lack of willingness of a team to show professional vulnerability, this makes complete sense. So, what is the answer? It is simply this: be clear about, and follow, your 'true north' – the tenets that are integral to you.

I know what you are thinking: how can we be authentic with such high stakes? There is no easy answer to this question, but I do think we can begin to unlock authenticity through courage. It might have to start with you, the Courageous Caveman, and you may have to role model it to your team – adults and pupils alike.

If enough teams can show bravery, we may then see it in an entire school staff. If enough schools have it, and here's the exciting and glorious bit, we might see the beginnings of a braver education system. I'm ever the Champion Caveman optimist! Why not, though? Surely something has to change. Anyway, let's get our feet back on the ground...

At the beginning of the chapter, I explained how my performance soared when working in a team where the members were completely comfortable with professional vulnerability. The question I'd like to address next is how the team came to acquire such comfort with this? What gives the team members their confidence and humility? The answer, in my opinion, is self-awareness. The chances are, they have done the inner work. And they may well have found their journey of self-awareness quite painful at times. After all, what right-minded person likes to look in the mirror at their own dysfunctions or shortcomings? Certainly not me!

The truth will set you free, but first it may piss you off.

Gloria Steinem – American feminist, journalist and social political activist

It takes courage to admit 'you don't know what you don't know'. Some members of the team might not know it, but as a result of the *inner work* they've most probably carried out over the years, they have done the hard yards and are comfortable with themselves and their place and role within the team.

The payoffs from successfully stepping up to the challenge of doing the inner work can be substantial, with strengthened self-control, discernment and increased empathy. This, in turn, should lead to improved teamwork, an aspect of Champion Caveman Culture that we have spoken about throughout this chapter and book.

Trinity of self-awareness: Know thyself, improve thyself and complement thyself

Anthony Tjan – entrepreneur, strategic adviser and venture investor

I spend a lot of my time helping colleagues through interpersonal conflicts. More often than not, they are experiencing frustration at the way they have been treated or spoken to. They often allude to the fact they are not alone, and that other staff have experienced similar treatment. I gently probe and ask if the offending person has ever been held to account for their behaviour. The response I frequently hear is, "No, they've been doing it for years and they don't realise the impact it has. It has gone on for so long now that it's harder to tackle."

Lack of self-awareness is often the root cause of these problems, and usually (and frustratingly) there are no quick fixes. I often catch myself smiling wryly as my coachees comment how helpful it would be if they could just say, "For goodness' sake, could you just please become more self-aware?" Suffice to say, I don't recommend this approach, particularly if the person upsetting other colleagues is more senior, which is so often the case.

Another interesting part of my career is working with colleagues who wish to explore self-control and strategies to manage triggers. The added challenge here is tiredness. It goes without saying that working in schools can be an emotionally wearing job. Managing emotional triggers when below par can be tricky at the best of times. That said, I continually marvel at teacher and leader resilience. During times when other folk may explode, educators can remain outwardly composed, even though on the inside they may be fit to burst!

Rather than react, Champion Cavemen will often respond impressively to situations. And for me, responding is a real skill. It requires you to pause mentally for a moment, stave off the temptation to react, manage your emotions and choose a more helpful path. This approach was so beautifully captured in the German proverb featured at the beginning of the chapter – *First think, then act.*

Without this type of self-control, staff can be held hostage by their own emotions, reacting with no filter to life around them. Obviously, this can present a real challenge to other members of the team, who may feel like they are treading on eggshells to maintain the peace.

> **Experience is not what happens to you; it's what you do with what happens to you.**
>
> Ken Blanchard – American author, business consultant and motivational speaker

As a skill, this is certainly one that I've had to work on, and it's one I'm still developing. On occasion, my impetuous nature will trump common sense and, before I know it, I've committed to a course of action that might not always be the most helpful. An ex-colleague, who was also a good friend, used to gently tease me about this tendency. One morning, upon arriving at my desk, I was greeted with a little note and a cup of tea. He had simply written:

TH...ACT...INK. Something to consider for your epitaph...

It took me a while, but when the penny dropped, I had a good belly laugh. He was absolutely right, of course, and had described one of my many idiosyncrasies to a tee. What he was saying, in his infinitely clever way, was that, on occasion, I can be guilty of acting before a thought has even had the opportunity to take its natural course – even before it has left my head! He would gently remind me that a chosen response can often yield a more fruitful outcome. He was great to work with, as he never took himself too seriously and often chuckled about his own leadership foibles, too.

The three As – Awareness, Acceptance, Action

In the instant impact world of education, developing self-awareness can be comparably slow. Whether you are developing it in yourself, or whether you are supporting someone else, be mindful that bringing about lasting change in yourself or others because of improved self-awareness can take months, even years.

If you are contemplating some inner work, it may be helpful to embrace the three As: Awareness, Acceptance and Action. This strikingly simple model was shared with me many years ago by a colleague who was attending Al-Anon Family Groups meetings.

Awareness

I am aware of my strengths, 'blind spots', triggers or motivators.

Acceptance

Even though it might be slightly uncomfortable to acknowledge this strength, 'blind spot', trigger or motivator, I fully accept that, currently, it is a part of me and who I am.

Action

Now that I am aware, and fully accept my strengths, 'blind spots', triggers or motivators, I can take action to manage them. This action will help me to minimise any negative impact or further strengthen the positive impact in my (professional) life.

In my experience, this beautifully simplistic model can be extremely effective.

When using the model, I like to acknowledge three key points:

1. It can sometimes be painful to accept certain characteristics. For some colleagues, denial may be an easier option. If you deny the existence of an unhelpful characteristic, you won't have to take action to manage it. Remember the pearl of wisdom in the earlier quote from Gloria Steinem?
2. No meaningful action can take place if acceptance hasn't been reached. Be gentle with yourself during the acceptance stage. Full acceptance may take months. Rushing this may hamper the impact of any action taken.
3. Keep taking action and ask for help from a trusted friend or colleague. The chances are that it may have taken a lifetime to cultivate an unhelpful characteristic, so it won't disappear with one action. You may need to keep working on yourself so that you don't revert to your default setting.

Everything that irritates us about others can lead us to an understanding of ourselves.

Carl Gustav Jung – one of the world's most influential psychiatrists

When covering self-awareness, it would be remiss of us not to touch on emotional intelligence, as the two go hand in hand.

Much has been written about the importance of emotional intelligence, which is often explained as comprising four areas:

1. Understanding your own emotions – self-awareness.
2. Understanding the emotions of others – social awareness.
3. Managing/regulating your own behaviour.
4. Managing relationships.

It goes without saying that, in the context of our book, the mastering of all four areas would be of great benefit in helping us to move in a positive direction along our continuum. If you are contemplating some inner work, perhaps the most useful starting place would be with the first point: understanding and recognising your own emotions. However, this can often be challenging, as we grapple with the difference between how we are perceived by others and our internal reality. For example, whilst you may see yourself as a shy person who is entirely comfortable in your own company, others may perceive you as gregarious and a people person. If you are mindful of this tension, can you take the necessary action to manage it accordingly?

We all present to the world in different ways. Sometimes, this creates a dichotomy between how others see us and how we see ourselves.

Caveman Consideration

Why not work on and improve your emotional intelligence? After all, this can be learnt.

Data collected from a study of over a million people by Dr Travis Bradberry, president of TalentSmart, a leading provider of emotional intelligence assessments and co-author of *Emotional Intelligence 2.0*, identified the nine behaviours of people with high emotional intelligence that help them succeed in life. Perhaps you could set some time aside with a colleague or your team and use our questions – which follow each of the nine points below – as a prompt for further reflection.

Behaviours of people with high emotional intelligence:

1. They focus on the positive, acknowledging what they can control (their own thinking) while remaining aware of those factors they can't. They invest their energy in the former and consciously choose not to waste energy on the latter.

   Question: How much time do you invest in the things you can't control?

2. They use an extensive emotional lexicon to decipher and master their feelings. For example, "I feel rubbish" versus "I feel anxious/ashamed/guilty/resentful."

   Question: How extensive is your emotional vocabulary?

3. They are neither passive nor aggressive but instead strike a healthy balance between the two and are assertive. The result? They can set healthy boundaries whilst remaining affable, which helps to ensure they don't upset people and can tackle conflict productively.

Question: Are there times when you are aggressive or passive? How can you move towards becoming more assertive?

4. They are genuinely interested in people. This is anchored in empathy; the more you care about those around you, the more inquisitive you are. When working in a team, it pays to be interested in others, as you can ensure that everyone is playing to their strengths – that they are, in the words of American author Jim Collins, "Sitting on the right seats."

   Question: How (appropriately!) curious are you?

5. They forgive but don't forget. They forgive because they understand the emotional demerits of holding a grudge, but they remember because they know it may help to guard against similar future scenarios.

   Question: How do you respond to difficult situations?

6. They understand that when you compare, you lose. Instead, they derive their worth from within. Whilst they are open to the views and opinions of others, they won't let these detract them from their own accomplishments or spoil their fun.

   Question: Do you allow others to 'rock your boat' and destabilise you? What actions can you take to keep yourself steady?

7. They seek to inject fun into everything they do, for themselves and for the people around them.

They understand that having fun can often take the heat out of a tricky situation.

Question: Where is the needle on your fun-o-meter?

8. They have a thicker skin as a result of their self-confidence and self-acceptance. It can be harder to rile a person with a higher EQ (emotional quotient).

Question: How easily offended are you?

9. They manage their negative inner voice and understand that it is made up of thoughts or feelings and not facts.

Question: How much airtime do you give to negative self-talk?

So, how do you shape up? Where do you need to do a little more inner work? Why not take these questions one at a time and chat them through with a trusted friend or colleague?

We can occasionally be left thinking, "Why do they think that about me?" In this situation, chatting things over with trusted friends or colleagues can often provide clarity, as we may do or say things unconsciously that only others can see. On occasion, someone I meet will misconstrue what I mean, which I find irksome. A little look in the mirror can reveal why, as I reflect on what I've said or how I have behaved. Effective teams are made up of people who attend to, and successfully manage, their self-awareness, both internally and how others view them.

Self-awareness isn't one truth. It's a delicate balance of two distinct, even competing, viewpoints

Tasha Eurich – organisational psychologist, researcher and
New York Times bestselling author

Showing Caveman courage in a high-stakes system is no mean feat; the audacity needed to be authentic and vulnerable is to be commended and will surely earn trust. But let's be clear: there are no quick wins in gaining greater self-awareness; it is a journey rather than a destination. However, if along the way, Caveman staff can muster the courage to show their brilliance and their vulnerabilities, then I would wager that a Champion Caveman Culture starts to become far more tenable.

Over to You

So, how can we cultivate self-awareness and develop a trusting Champion Caveman Culture where vulnerability is not only welcomed but seen as a strength?

1. Know yourself – strengths and 'blind spots'

If you know yourself, you can be more authentic. The more authentic you are, the more trust you can build. (Remember Frances Frei's 'wobble'?)

Plan to ameliorate your self-awareness through:

   a. Self-assessment activities. There are many self-assessment tools out there, including the Myers-Briggs Type Indicator (MBTI), DISC and the Kolbe Index, to name a few.

b. Regular and planned feedback from colleagues and friends (360 assessments), which help to inform external self-awareness. Sometimes, this feedback can make for difficult reading, but it is all grist to the mill. I can vividly recall receiving some feedback years ago that described me as overly idealistic. I took it to heart and spent some time working through it, especially as I got stuck at the Acceptance stage in the three As model. However, on reflection, I now know that the feedback was correct. I am now mindful of this characteristic and take action to manage it accordingly.

2. Mirror the behaviours of people with a higher EQ

Take another look at the nine behaviours of people with strong emotional intelligence. Do you have friends or colleagues with a high EQ? Why not have a go at replicating their behaviours?

3. Practice makes progress

Utilising new behaviours gained through improved self-awareness is like learning to drive. Initially, you must consciously think about every action. With practice, it requires less thought, becoming increasingly automatic until it takes the form of an engrained habit. So, keep practising your new emotionally intelligent behaviours. When you do this, your brain will naturally stop referencing old, unhelpful behaviours, which will become consigned to the history books of your mind.

On a practical level, if you have completed a personality test that has unearthed some helpful awareness, commit yourself to action and share your plan with a trusted colleague or friend. Ask them to hold you to account or, at the very least, provide them with regular progress updates.

Why not try a self-assessment test as a team? Often, these exercises generate a personality report. Share and discuss your own with other members of the team and get to know each other better. This is a fun, non-threatening bonding exercise that can work particularly well with newly formed teams.

If you decide to try some new behaviours resulting from the report, why not share them with other members of the team? You can then all meet at regular points during the year to provide progress updates.

Through understanding our colleagues better, we can get to know what makes them tick. It is all too easy to get irritated or annoyed with our Caveman colleagues, but why not scratch beneath the surface with a self-assessment test and take the time to find out what is going on with them? When I am tired and getting frustrated with someone, I will often lean on the following quote, which introduces a helpful element of compassion: "If we knew all, we would forgive all."

In my experience, and as previously mentioned, self-aware teams are a joy to belong to. It is likely that they:

- Can resolve conflict more smoothly.
- Enjoy working with each other more.
- Exercise better judgement.
- Are more comfortable with embracing their intuition.

4. Use coaching

In Chapter Eight, we discussed the merits of asking more and telling less and explained that coaching can be an effective tool in helping Caveman staff feel more empowered. We also took some time to explain the structure of coaching and how we might strive to ensure that our coachees develop greater clarity of thinking in relation to:

- Knowledge of self – in particular, their own strengths.
- Understanding of others – including their words, actions and motives.

It is, therefore, easy to see that coaching and self-awareness are a natural fit and can work hand in hand. Regular coaching sessions can be a highly effective tool in helping coachees to unlock potential through increased self-awareness.

Chapter 10

Playtime

In this chapter, we'll explore pausing, playtime, perfectionism and performance.

> **Play is the royal road to childhood happiness and adult brilliance.**
>
> Michael Mendizza – entrepreneur, educator, author and documentary filmmaker

 OVER TO DAVE...

As we near the end of our Caveman adventure, I want to use this chapter as a pause point, where you can stop for a moment and consider all that has been written so far. This is an opportunity to explore which bits might be relevant to your Caveman contexts, and which bits you can leave for now. It's a chance for you to savour the parts you've enjoyed and a further opportunity to chew over the more complex parts that resonate, and which may be useful as an approach in the future.

If you've read the book with a colleague, or as a team, it would be nice to think that you could make a pot of tea (or perhaps something stronger – maybe a large Vimto on the rocks, depending how the mood takes you), grab a packet of your favourite biscuits (the chosen superfood of all teachers) and sit down together for maybe an hour (yes, sixty minutes, nobody is watching) and just engage in unstructured professional dialogue. Save for Chapter Seven (The Intermission), we haven't really provided you with any thinking time – it's been all go...

How can we expect you to start developing Champion Caveman Culture if we don't provide you with the time and the space to think about, and plan for, the changes you want to make? This chapter is literally Playtime. The metaphorical morning bell has rung, and you've got your milk and a handful of Heroes out of the tin. As we all know, teacher creativity spikes when we're a little less congested, so ensure your marking is up to date, your planning is done and your desk is clear. Through playtime, we invite our creative urges to bubble to the fore, ready to be harnessed and then unleashed.

You see, the Caveman brain needs time to catch up; the subconscious mind needs the space and time to order and sort what has been ingested. This time is not wasted time, nor is it coasting time. It doesn't mean we're not focused – on the contrary. It is during this time that we can have unexpected moments of epiphany and gain greater clarity. It can be 'the royal road to childhood happiness and adult brilliance'. It can provide the energy and the capacity to feel excitement about a new idea to trial. We have the time to foster motivation and feel that sense of adventure and playfulness at the prospect of where things might lead.

This chapter is a 'non-chapter' about the virtues, and indeed the necessity, of non-directed time – or playtime, as we call it. In simple terms, it is about standing back, downing tools and smelling the roses. Moreover, it is a chapter in which we alert you to the enemies of playtime: those factors, things or thinking that can erode or even prevent playtime from happening. Can you imagine if we removed playtimes for our pupils? If we simply ploughed on, teaching them new concepts, skills and knowledge, lesson after lesson? You will recall the notion of Caveman congestion in the early chapters... maybe playtime is the laxative!

You see, by giving others – and yourself – the permission and the opportunity to slow down and enjoy a little slice of playtime, you are allowing yourself and, more importantly, your colleagues time to connect, consider, reflect and question practice beyond the everyday, well-trodden path. You move your colleagues away from passive inclusion in the 'already decided' towards active participation in a possible new future.

So, I'd like to commit some time to raising our awareness of those factors that can interfere with, curtail or even prevent our playtime. If we know what they are, we can act to better manage them. For me, the obvious starting point is how we better manage or temper the unrelenting pace of change in schools and education (see Chapter Five – True North); the constant striving for excellence that can rob us of time to reflect, to embed our practice and, dare I say it, can prevent us from finding contentment, as we scurry, or even sprint, to achieve the next pressing target or external validation.

I could be wrong, but it appears that we may have normalised this relentless pursuit of excellence in our profession, and, in doing so, have eroded or cast doubt on the value of playtime. Even worse, we may feel a sense of discomfort or guilt if we let the speedometer needle drop below 100mph; possibly because it can sometimes feel that any speed between 80mph and 99mph, while still eclipsing a reasonable approach to any work/life balance, is coasting. Some of us may well feel discomfort or unease that, at 80mph, we have some thinking time and, heaven forbid, rare pangs of contentedness (which, by the way, will still require work to maintain).

I can distinctly recall this very sensation as a headteacher following a successful external validation. In the years running up to this point, the speedometer rarely dropped below 110mph. It went on, day after day, week after week and year after year in a seemingly relentless journey. It became our norm. The visitors came and went, and we were left with a very complimentary visit report affirming much of the team's previous hard work. Surely it was time to take a breather, savour the moment and consolidate everything that had been achieved to date? Surely it was time for staff to enjoy the fruits of their efforts, shift down a gear and metaphorically take their foot off the accelerator? We could now afford to be travelling at 80mph, couldn't we? After all, we'd earnt it.

The reality of that period, for me, was very different. It was a time in which I felt the pangs of guilt that we were no longer travelling at breakneck speed. I worried that we were enjoying the next, and different, part of our journey, even though it was no less important. I was anxious that we were drifting – maybe even towards contentment. In the course of my work, I often speak to colleagues who experience this sensation, and, whilst it is comforting to know it isn't just me, it is still concerning that the system is such that this phenomenon is commonplace.

Connectedness is a way of thinking described as looking inward to the internal rhythms of the self. It involves asking life's bigger questions to gain clarity, insight and wisdom. Understanding ourselves is to be able to give sense and purpose to life and can be recognised via learners' questioning, trying, challenging, testing and experimenting.

Miriam Tanti – educator and an advocate of a 'Slow' approach to education (and life)

Teachers and leaders may even entertain the unhelpful self-talk that dares to suggest 80mph is the speed of complacency. I couldn't resist typing the word complacency into Google. It describes it as a 'feeling of smug or uncritical satisfaction with oneself or one's achievements'. This literally made me howl with laughter, as I recalled the plethora of occasions when I have asked colleagues to talk positively about their educational roles and their achievements, with the aim of helping them to see what an extraordinary job they do.

Correct me if I am wrong, but the teaching profession, because of the extreme negativity bias, is one of the most humble, self-effacing, non-complacent professions on earth. In our world, even phenomenal achievements are played down or normalised. If you don't believe me, tune into the annual National Teaching Awards on the BBC and listen to the acceptance speeches. They all start in the same fashion, stating that this is an award for all the teachers and children in their school, implying that it has nothing, or very little, to do with them, which is, of course, simply not true. Quite how the word complacency has even appeared near our profession is one of the great mysteries of the universe. I would say that if staff feel complacent, they have got the balance right. Our understanding of this word bears little resemblance to the mainstream understanding.

It is sad, and indeed frustrating, that the notion of contentment can be viewed by some as a state in which there is a lack of ambition or aspiration. We believe that this isn't true. Achieving and remaining in a state of contentment needs maintenance. In fact, it is a state that needs striving for, and it's worth every moment you invest; it could well be the very thing that helps to catalyse a cultural change for the better. It provides an opportunity for staff to catch their breath and enjoy a more meaningful, long-lasting state of readiness and application. It is from this state of contentedness that, we believe, the gate can open to Champion Caveman Culture.

In achieving a hard-fought team goal, many of us feel a huge sense of relief, after which we may experience a period of exhaustion as we begin to relax and reflect on the blood, sweat and tears that have been required. So often in this period, staff can be loaded up with the next goal. It is easy to see why, if this happens, they may react less than positively. These points in time are important cultural junctures and, in our opinion, if they are to be harnessed positively, they need to be managed carefully. To this end, it is crucial that staff are given the time for the exhaustion to pass, which will enable the relief to transform into joy and, ultimately, for the joy to become pride. With energy replenished and pride fully intact, staff may edge further along the continuum.

Caveman Consideration

Taking time out to 'smell the roses', appreciate what we have or what is working well, is a useful way to spend playtime.

Here are some questions that can help you do this:

- Can we build on or further strengthen existing successful practices? Linked to this: where and how can we replicate successful practice?

- How often do we take the time to pause and smell the roses?

- When we have all been working hard to reach a team or school goal, and we achieve what we set out to accomplish, do we savour the moment and really take the time to understand each and every ingredient of our success? In doing so, we can consciously replicate this process.

I would hazard a guess and say that staff, as a rule, do not build in a huge amount of time to pause, step back and really appreciate their professional team achievements or successes. Let's take a moment to flip this on its head. Imagine, if you will, that a school development target has been missed. In response, a school will often be forensic in its approach to investigating the possible causes and work relentlessly to mitigate against a similar thing happening in the future. The missed target might also appear in the appraisal process or within the school development plan. In short, the energy and focus that is directed by staff to address missed targets is quite something to behold. No stone will be left unturned or door unknocked.

Let's now imagine that for a number of years, the very same school has been working tirelessly as a team towards a shared goal. The team has performed exceptionally and, as a result, outcomes have improved markedly. The school's achievement is externally validated, and the team are proud beyond belief. It is quite a moment in the journey of the school. What's important to note here is that the success is no accident. It is the result of clear-sighted strategy, team empowerment and deliberate leadership practice. The ingredients for success were vast and complex, but every step was planned for and meticulously executed.

So, in much the same way that the school was forensic in its response to a missed target, do you think it will commit the same amount of time and energy to understanding its success? Will it put aside time for a comprehensive understanding of its strengths, ensuring that this triumph can be replicated in different areas going forward? I think we all know the answer to these questions: sadly, probably not. And, in not taking the time to reflect and understand its success, a huge opportunity or gift is missed. Gone is the chance to recognise, celebrate and acknowledge the tireless work of staff (and really savour and bask in this). Gone is the chance to thank staff individually for the part they played, and gone is the confidence this builds and the togetherness it fosters. The staff won't feel the benefit of having their hard-fought gains celebrated publicly. It is beyond sad that these cultural pearls can sometimes be overlooked, and the moment lost forever.

I am always puzzled by how schools can gloss over and play down such phenomenal achievements whilst any miniscule, missed target will be explored to within an inch of its life. I believe this is the consequence of the extreme negativity bias in action. It would seem that savouring the moment in our current climate will almost always be trumped by the need to crack on and achieve the next target or external accolade.

One should never, but never, pass by an opportunity to celebrate.

David Malouf – one of Australia's greatest writers

What exactly is it in our thinking that makes us crowd out playtime?

Before we attempt to answer this question, I just want to be clear; I am not for one second advocating that we should be any less ambitious or aspirational for our pupils, schools and system. Neither am I suggesting we set a course for complacency or even mediocrity – far from it. I just think we could be healthier in our professional striving. Let me explain what I mean...

Let's start by exploring a phrase I hear a lot: *'the relentless pursuit of excellence'*. The word 'relentless' here, for me, is unhelpful. If you were to pick up a thesaurus and look for alternatives, amongst others you'd find these words: 'unyielding', 'single-minded', 'unforgiving'... I think you get the picture. It sounds like come hell or high water, nothing will stop it. It seems to dehumanise what would otherwise be a perfectly laudable aspiration. It can sometimes seem that the relentless pursuit of excellence is simply concerned with the achievement of one external goal after another, with little time between for playtime, to enjoy the journey, appreciate the success or breathe in those roses. As soon as one goal is achieved, the planning starts for the next one, even if the previous goal was hard-earned and stretched over a number of years, taking an emotional and physical toll on the team in the process.

Caveman Consideration

Could there be another way – a balance between healthy striving and an appreciation of what is working effectively? Could schools focus on tackling deficits for half a term or six weeks and then focus on understanding and replicating strength and success for the next six weeks? Could this pattern be repeated in the spring and summer terms, thus providing an equal balance of tackling deficits and understanding strengths or success?

Could this help our Caveman staff along the continuum towards a more contented state, and maybe even beyond?

Managing the desire to be perfect: is good, good enough?

Yes, we think it can be. (And just to be clear; the use of the word 'good' in this context is in no way linked to an inspectoral judgement.)

Another unhelpful, and sometimes unacknowledged, external pressure on staff and schools comes from society. It is of little surprise that our Cynical Caveman can feel exhausted and anxious in a society preoccupied with being the very best in all areas, at all times. The pressure to have the perfect relationship, the perfect body or to be the perfect parent seems unrelenting. Oh, and whilst you're working on those areas, don't forget to be blissfully content, too! #ImNotPerfectButImWorkingOnIt

As a teacher and leader, I certainly felt this expectation in my professional role, too. And, in my mind, rightfully so. With the life chances of children in my hands, nothing less than the best was acceptable. For me, 'good enough' was certainly not setting the bar high enough. Surely my pupils and the community deserved more.

If, in a rare moment, I did dare to accept, or entertain the notion, that good was good enough in my teaching or leadership, I simply had to pick up an educational publication or listen to the news and, as sure as eggs is eggs, I would hear or read about a world-class education system, an educational centre of excellence or another proud outstanding setting. Within seconds, my standards were recalibrated and I was reminded that simply being good was shy of the mark. I decided that I must do better, never mind the cost to my pupils, my staff or to me. Like many other Caveman colleagues, I subliminally acknowledged, without question, that simply being good was ordinary and *not* enough. On reflection, I now question the helpfulness of that judgement.

Over recent years, there has been a discernible shift in my outlook and approach, and I'm not entirely certain why. I have started to warm to the idea that good is indeed good enough. Surely to remain good takes some effort and thinking, and to remain contented takes some work, too? Just because we have reached a goal, doesn't mean that we can stop trying to maintain it.

In an effort to try and understand the change in my outlook, I began to do some research and explore why my engrained thinking and approach may not have served me, and others, as well as I may have thought.

The idea that good is good enough was introduced in the 1950s by a paediatrician called Donald Winnicott, who made quite a stir in the parenting arena. In a nutshell, he contended that a 'good enough' mother was more effective than a perfect one. He described a good enough mother as honest, well-intentioned and the provider of unconditional love. He went on to explain the downsides of striving to be the perfect mother. Winnicott's work, all those years ago, seems more relevant now than ever, and it got me thinking about my own leaning towards perfectionism, which you will recall me mentioning in the earlier part of this book. Much of the research in this area suggests that an over-emphasis on perfectionism may be caused by parents failing to provide their children with sufficient affirmation, or alternatively, children internalising their parents' impossibly high standards. I'm not convinced that either applies to me, but the fact is, I am still prone to imposing high standards on myself. Annoyingly so.

Caveman Nuggets

Good is good enough.

In my opinion, one thing is strikingly clear: over the years, the extreme negativity bias has amplified my perfectionism, and I'm convinced it has done the same for many other colleagues, too. Whilst I wasn't short of parental affirmation, professional affirmation in my developmental years as a teacher certainly wasn't free flowing. If you couple this with a system that focuses almost exclusively on the negative, or the 'gaps', you will begin to see why the need for perfection permeated many aspects of my professional life.

I guess I should be a little gentler on myself. When I look more closely at who I was trying to be perfect for, I feel proud that it was for my pupils, my staff and my community. I was not aiming to be perfect in the eyes of an external body. In fact, I remember being very deliberate about choosing the superlatives to aim for: 'exceptional' or 'first class' were a couple of my favourites. I can also recall being very clear about the words I *wouldn't* use when self-evaluating our work. The use of words synonymous with judgement may have led to a watering down of our shared vision or, even worse, the striving towards someone else's goal. As a leader, I only ever wanted our school community to be exceptional in the eyes of our parents, staff and pupils. For me, these are the groups that really matter, and I know this rings true for Bob and his schools, too.

Whilst ruminating on this subject, it occurred to me that perhaps my understanding of perfectionism was too simplistic and, therefore, unhelpful. Perhaps it would be more useful to consider two types of perfectionism: excellence-seeking perfectionism, which can be useful in achieving performance gains, and failure-avoiding perfectionism, which is underpinned by the fear of making mistakes. It is clear to me that the extreme negativity bias is synonymous with the latter. The three parts of Chapter Six cover this substantially and highlight the tendency of staff to focus constantly on the negatives or deficits, while working tirelessly to eradicate them. Typically, the overriding focus is on *how* they are doing and not *what* they are doing, which in the longer term may not be for the best.

What's more, failure-avoiding perfectionism may also be responsible for Caveman staff experiencing the strong inclination to procrastinate, as they feel they are unable to achieve tasks perfectly. Essentially, they won't take part in a race they can't win. Consumed by the self-imposed requirement for the outcome of the task to be 'just so', staff may lose sight of productivity, suitability and timeframes.

Don't get me wrong, perfectionism can certainly have its place. Heaven forbid that I should fall ill and need brain or heart surgery. With such exacting requirements, and such little room for error, I would hope that my surgeon was a perfectionist to the nth degree. My life would depend on it. The phrase 'life and death' is absolutely fitting in this context. (With this in mind, I would be quite surprised if I saw a mission statement over the entrance to the brain surgery department that read, *Good is Good Enough*.)

So, let's take a moment to step back and reflect. Yes, I acknowledge that educating our younger generation is one of society's most important roles. As I've explained, we have the life chances of young people in our hands. What could be more important? Those of us in pastoral roles will have to manage some incredibly challenging situations that relate directly to the safeguarding of pupils and, sadly, these may well be life and death scenarios.

However, for the most part, our roles, while hugely important, do not hinge on life and death decisions. In light of this, I can begin to see why I have recently started to empathise with the view that good is indeed good enough.

Understanding the difference between healthy striving and perfectionism is critical to picking up your life. Research shows that perfectionism hampers success. In fact, it's often the path to depression, anxiety, addiction and life paralysis.

Brené Brown – American research professor, lecturer and author

This quote makes a significant and sobering point indeed. Notice any resemblance with the characteristics of our Cynical Caveman?

So, as both teachers and leaders, how can we successfully navigate our respective career paths and ensure healthy striving? I would strongly suggest looking inwards or undertaking some inner work (see Chapter Nine). With increased self-awareness, we can better marshal our thoughts, feelings and drivers. If perfection is the goal or driver, it comes with a stark health warning, as its foundations are reliant on looking outwards for affirmation.

Healthy striving is self-focused: How can I improve? Perfectionism is other-focused: What will they think?

Brené Brown

As I've previously mentioned, some of my most clear-sighted and creative moments happen during the school holidays. I assume this is because I am not on my giant hamster wheel and can enjoy the head space that gives my imagination the chance to play and dream. This is a space where I can join up the dots and make connections. So, during term time, make sure you factor in some 'holiday-mode time', during which your brain, and the brains of your team, can do their thing.

Ding-a-ling – it's playtime!

Over to You

With Brené Brown's words in mind, as you enjoy your cuppa and your favourite biscuit, take time to ponder the areas that demand your close focus and those that you can proudly take time to appreciate and embed. Maybe even afford yourself a sense of well-earned complacency as you edge closer to becoming a Contented or even a Champion Caveman.

Chapter 11
Time For a Change

Most of the old moles I know wish they had listened less to their fears and more to their dreams.

From *The Boy, the Mole, the Fox and the Horse* by Charlie Mackesy
– British illustrator and author

 OVER TO BOB AND DAVE...

So, here we are at the end of our EduCaveman journey. We feel privileged to have been able to share our book with you. Thank you for reading it and for staying the course. As mentioned in the Aperitif, we hope that, if nothing else, you have been reminded of your excellent career choice and reflected on the joy and the inspiration that your job can bring. We want this book to have enabled you to let go of the daily hustle and bustle and any current wobbles you may be feeling and examine, possibly even reignite, your passion for this truly exceptional profession.

Moreover, we sincerely hope that the book has provided you with a chance to reflect and understand more fully the crucial role that you and your school play in inspiring youngsters from a multitude of backgrounds and starting points in life, whilst also creating thriving, connected communities up and down the country. After all, what other job allows you to influence a child's behaviour and their strengths, help with their weaknesses and nurture their creativity and imagination? Although, sometimes, we won't ever know the influence and inspiration we have provided, just knowing that we are making a difference makes it all feel worthwhile.

We also hope our book has given you a sense of perspective, some time to pinpoint where you are and then where your school is. We know that some schools will have already started their cultural journey and will be 'on the bus', with the radio tuned in to their desired frequency and their 'true north' set. Others may just be starting to plan their cultural expedition. There may even be some schools that are yet to discover and acknowledge the power and potential of cultural development. Given that education can often be cluttered and overburdened with the next best initiative, this is hardly surprising.

Frankly, it doesn't matter where you find yourself because what we are advocating, and have been throughout this book, is not a cultural *revolution* led by your good self and a well-armed band of like-minded individuals, but a cultural *evolution*, or an 'edu-lution', as we like to call it. This is an approach that begins from where you – and the school – find yourself on the EduCaveman Continuum. It's a steady, systematic approach to school development from a cultural perspective, and it can be entirely done at your own pace – softly, softly catchee monkey! It is indeed time for a change. It is time to listen to your dreams about the school you really want and to realise that the solutions to the challenges you face may well lie within the expertise of your staff. So, resist the temptation to look outwards and instead embrace and harness the magic within.

Our raison d'être for writing this book was to encourage educators to consider how they may further strengthen their moral purpose, taking small steps, or even large ones, towards addressing the negativity bias that might exist within them or their school and creating the conditions in which the fantastic people in our profession can hang onto the feeling of raw excitement that first drew them to the world of education. This is a world where hope, optimism, positivity and the very best in the human spirit reside. It's where our forgotten saints quietly go about their business, achieving extraordinary things daily for the communities they serve.

As we explained earlier in the book, our aim was never to provide you with a precise list of instructions and next steps, nor was it to deliver an array of prepacked strategies to add to the list of the ones you have tried already. You are far better placed to decide on these. After all, you are the experts in your respective settings. We were always, and still are, more concerned with providing you with a metaphorical kitchen and lots of equipment, ideas and ingredients for creating your own menu. And remember, unlike *MasterChef*, it is up to you how you complete the menu – there is no limit on time or on the number of contestants that can join in to help you. This is a cultural recipe book for all members of the school community, from the head chef through to the sous-chef. So, let's get cooking!

Although this is sadly the end for us, it really is the beginning for you. What you choose to do with what we've imparted lies in your hands, but we hope it will be the start of a great edu-adventure. Imagine the collective power if all Caveman colleagues answered the call to arms; the call to rediscover joy...

All Yours

So, here we are at a cultural crossroads. It's not so much 'over to you' but more 'all yours'. If the Nuggets, Considerations and ideas within the chapters of our book have whet your appetite for a spot of planned and deliberate cultural investment, then you best get cracking! That said, whilst there might be some quick wins that help to nudge you in a positive direction along the EduCaveman Continuum, this is a slow game. Meaningful, deep-routed cultural transformation is a process that can take years. And our sincere hope is that these roots will help to alleviate congestion, nourish discretionary effort and bring more contentment and joy to the jobs you do. Moreover, we hope that through exploring and playing with the ideas in our book, you can lessen the impact of the negativity bias.

We simply ask that you take what you like and leave the rest. Get the kettle on, pop the lid off the cake tin, assemble the troops and grab the sugar paper. Let's do what educators do best and brainstorm our journey…

"What do you think is the biggest waste of time?"
"Comparing yourself to others," said the mole.
"I wonder if there is a school of unlearning?"

From *The Boy, the Mole, the Fox and the Horse*

Ciao for Now...

Want to know more?

Why not visit the EduCaveman website:
www.EduCaveman.co.uk

Want Bob and Dave to work with you and/or your team?

They speak at INSETs and facilitate workshops and seminars. Their content can be tailored to meet your requirements, and their sessions are always:

- ✓ Guaranteed to motivate
- ✓ Full of practical tools and strategies
- ✓ Engaging
- ✓ Thought-provoking
- ✓ Guaranteed to bring greater clarity
- ✓ A valuable opportunity for participants to reflect on developing their practice

Email: **bobtwells1@gmail.com**

or

Email: **dave@shineeducationandtraining.co.uk**

If you would prefer to have a chat, please either call:

Bob **+44 (0) 7940 447681**

or

Dave **+44 (0) 7979 851703**

National Trainers of the Year

Bob and Dave were awarded the title of Trainers of the Year in the 2019 NASBTT (National Association of School-Based Teacher Training) Awards. This award recognises excellence in school-based teacher education and the exceptionally hardworking and talented professionals involved in driving the profession.

In awarding the Trainer of the Year prize, the judging panel, comprising education and ITT experts, said: "Many of the nominees were evidently inspirational trainers in diverse aspects of initial teacher education, whose impact on the thinking and practice of significant numbers of trainee teachers is clearly apparent, but Dave and Bob are clearly a dynamic duo." As one judge commented, 'Their sessions are described in such a way (and evaluated incredibly highly by a range of trainees past and present) that one wants to book to attend.' The SCITT leaders say in their nomination that, 'We have been inundated with nomination requests from past and present trainees.' As one grateful recipient's testimonial said, 'I just had to say how fantastic the behaviour management training was today. They were the perfect training duo – hilarious at times and with so much good content. I certainly left feeling uplifted and with plenty of strategies to try.'

Acknowledgements

This book has taken nearly three years to reach you and has, on more than the odd occasion, been derailed by the global pandemic. But we made it – just.

We would firstly like to thank our long-suffering wives, Victoria and Gillian, for their tolerance, creative genius and insight, and for going the distance (and for pretending to care about colons and semi colons). You always found time to listen to us, even when you were both snowed under yourselves.

We'd also like to give special mention to our children, whom we love very much; we know that sometimes the book trumped our time and that you missed out. You have our solemn promise there won't be a sequel!

We'd like to express our gratitude to Rob Murray, our cartoonist, for bringing our words to life and for setting the satirical tone with such clever imagery. Your patience and innate ability to get inside our heads was remarkable. Even when we couldn't articulate what we wanted, you nailed it – and sometimes in seconds!

Didi, thank you so much for your help with the book's website and with filming. You're such fun to work with and nothing was too much trouble. Georgia, thank you for your wisdom and guidance in relation to technical aspects of the website. Had we been left in charge of this aspect we both know what would have happened! We'd like to express our thanks to George Russell, who, at the end of several long weeks, attempted to explain, amongst other things, search engine optimisation and meta tags – phrases we'd read about, but had no clear idea how to manage. Thank the lord you assumed control and tended to this area; we're very grateful.

To our social media marketing man – Tom Baker – we'd like to express our appreciation. Thank you for the ease with which you understood the essence of our book, as well as both your patience and warmth on Zoom calls. We promise to get better at social media...

We'd like to thank our copy editor and publisher, Danielle Wrate, for making our book eminently more readable. Your turn of phrase is effortlessly exquisite. We're also very grateful to the hawk eyes of Wendy Reed, our proofreader, and to Alexa Whitten, for doing an exceptional job with the internal layout of the book.

We're indebted to Margaret Hope for bringing the book alive with a breathtakingly bold front cover design – you are gifted, and we love it. We haven't forgotten the promise of a curry...

We'd like to give sincere thanks to our merry band of editors – all teachers, school leaders or retired educators – who gave up their precious time to read the first draft. We were both deeply touched by the time you gave and the quality of your feedback and suggestions for improvements. We took great heart from your contributions, and it kept us both truly motivated in the more challenging pandemic times. Thank you, Alexis Conway, Jo Payne, Rachel Barton, Rachel Nunns, Ian Holmes, Jonny Wackrill, Jill Dean, Guy Perkins, Marian Jones and Sue Winterton.

We would like to extend our penultimate thank you to Sir John Jones, for providing us with those much-needed 'pick me ups' at the more intense times in our respective careers – either in person or via YouTube. Thanks for taking the time to read our book and for your heartfelt feedback.

Last and by no means least, we'd like to thank every single educator who has listened to us talk about the contents of our book and provided us with encouragement, grounded insight and, above all else, kept us reminded of why we wrote it.